MW00412807

THIS IS HOW I

---

7 STRATEGIES TO ACCELERATE YOUR LEADERSHIP GROWTH AND PROMOTABILITY

SEAN OLSON

This book is dedicated to the glory of
God who makes all things possible.

Contents

Introduction - Role On   1

1   Strategy #1 - Uncover the Human Element   9

2   Strategy #2 - Manage Processes. Lead People.   19

3   Strategy #3 - Practice People Whispering   29

4   Strategy #4 - Win with T.E.A.M.   41

5   Strategy #5 - Learn the New Scorecard   53

6   Strategy #6 - Lead with Intention   65

7   Strategy #7 - Sustain Success with Coaching   77

8   Still Role-ing On   87

Introduction - Role On!

Bobby is like most aspiring leaders today. He is intelligent. He has a great education. He has opportunities to flex his leadership muscle. As a result, he has moved up the ladder rather quickly. He has moved so fast that he has hit a snag. His weaknesses are more apparent, and they are limiting his success at higher levels.

Through our coaching sessions, Bobby came to the awareness that the Bobby his friends and family loved was not the same Bobby that was showing up at work. He had always been known as a devoted, loving and fun friend, husband and father. Those close to him appreciated his care and his selflessness to help out anyone.

Yet, at work, Bobby was viewed as aloof, difficult to get to know, pushy, and bit arrogant. How could these two Bobbies exist? Were his friends and family wrong in their impression of him? Were his colleagues and direct reports wrong in their impressions? Once Bobby had the answer to these questions, he could think about what he needed to do to change. Perceptions are real, and they are incredibly difficult to change. If Bobby wanted to succeed at higher levels, he was going to have to make some changes.

Through our work together, Bobby was able to make some major changes in how he leads, and as a result, he is now connecting and executing at a much higher level. He takes the time to acknowledge his colleagues and their ideas. He is careful to listen and not respond immediately. He takes time to walk around offices and get to know people on a personal level. He even opened up about his own family and shared personal stories. His colleagues' perception of him has changed. It has come into alignment with how Bobby's loved ones see him. He is a better leader and others are now following. The tag of "interim" has been removed from his title, and he is now in his new role as a director.

The lessons and strategies about leadership and humanity Bobby learned accelerated his leadership development and set him up for success. As you too will discover in this book, Bobby learned how to uncover the human element. He used the strategy of people whispering and saw the results. He was intentional in his leadership and coaching. His leadership growth accelerated and his team is benefiting. These strategies will do the same for you.

Leadership. When it is missing, mayhem follows. When it is present, lives are changed.

You are starting a journey today. As you read these pages, you are beginning a journey in developing a deeper understanding of yourself and discovering key strategies to accelerate your leadership development and get promoted faster.

This is a journey into your humanity. It is a journey:
- into why leadership is about the *who*, not the *what*.
- to set others up for success in a way that you, as a leader, succeed simultaneously.
- to your inner greatness by pulling out the greatness in others.

The names of our clients have been changed for this book. They are all real stories and our clients are happy to share them. Because the stories highlight others on their team and their organizations, their real names and company names are not listed.

The following pages are the result of years of making mistakes. I have had more than my share of mistakes. Some were dramatic errors and some were blunders that hurt others. I have had the opportunity to coach hundreds of leaders that are making mistakes. These leaders span multiple sectors and levels in organizations. There are common traits that run through each of these leaders because, at the heart of it, they are people. We are all in the people business. No matter your role in an organization or life, if you are leader, it is about people.

Throughout my 25-year professional career, I have been blessed to work alongside incredible people. I have sat one-on-one with others and walked through the messes of life. I have had the opportunity to coach them and see them reach their version of success. It has been a pleasure to speak publicly to crowds as small as five and as large as over a thousand. Each of these moments have been opportunities to speak truth and offer challenges for personal and professional growth.

Renogize Professional Coaching has put together a team of coaches that serve clients around the country. Our team has experience working with start-ups all the way to Fortune 500 companies. We have had clients in higher education, non-profit, manufacturing, IT, government and many more. The strategies in this book transcend sector and experience. It is leadership, it is about people, and it works.

Over seventy percent of the leaders our company has worked with are in a new role. Research by Gallup indicates that forty percent of leaders in a new role fail. The sixty percent that make it are not necessarily effective; they just have not failed. With coaching and development, we have found that percentage of success and effectiveness can be much higher. Maximizing the opportunity of a new role and the details of the transition sets leaders up for success.

Forty-two percent of our clients are promoted during or within one year of their coaching engagements. This may seem counterintuitive. If seventy percent of our clients are recently in new roles, how are so many being promoted? Because they are being promoted *again* in a short period of time. Why does this happen? Because they are coachable, and coaching is the great accelerator.

That is the power of coaching. That is what effective coaching accomplishes. That was the driver in coming up with the name of our company: Renogize Professional Coaching.

Seven years ago, I was sitting at the dinner table with my wife, Jen, and our then seven-year-old daughter, Sydney. I had been advised by a colleague that when devising a name for our company, we should combine two words and create a new word. When doing so, URLs are typically available. So, we sat down and started talking.

To help our daughter understand, we used an analogy from HGTV, a television channel we enjoyed watching as a family. I explained that coaching is like the *renovation* of a house. The bones of the structure are good and the foundation is solid. After some additional walls, new fixtures, and a coat of paint, everything looks different and better. In coaching, we work to pull the best out of people and rearrange things. It is a new and improved version of themselves.

I also shared that coaching is *energizing*. Sometimes clients need a pat on the back. Sometimes they need trust and encouragement. Sometimes they need a swift kick in the butt to get going. We help charge their batteries and energize them to push past their limits.

My wife and daughter looked at one another and said, "Renovate and energize…RENOGIZE." We pulled out the laptop, went to GoDaddy and bought the URLs on the spot. When you involve the key people in your life, especially children, incredible things result.

Everyone can benefit from coaching that renovates and energizes, even you. Let's get more specific. Is this book for *you*?

- If you have been recently promoted and you want to capitalize on your new opportunity, this book is for you.
- If you are a leader looking to promote someone, this book is for you *and* that individual(s).

- If you wonder why promotion after promotion keeps passing you by, this book is for you.
- If you are a spouse, parent, child or friend (yes, that means YOU), this book is for you.

How can coaching span all of these needs? Because in the end, leadership is about *you*. Like Bobby, your leadership strength will grow as you become aware of who you are, how others see you, and how specific behaviors lead to those perceptions. It is about you being fully aware of how you were created and tapping into your brilliance. Once you learn to lead yourself successfully, you can lead others successfully. After tapping into your own brilliance, you will be ready to tap into the brilliance of others. Your role at work is critical. Your role at home is crucial. Your role as a human being and the potential to impact the world around you is unbelievable.

Here is what you can expect in the pages that follow. You will learn the 7 Strategies that will accelerate your leadership growth and promotability.

1. Learn how to **Uncover the Human Element**.
2. Understand the differences in **Managing Processes and Leading People**.
3. Discover the power of **People Whispering**.
4. Find how to **Win with T.E.A.M.**
5. Know how to master the **New Scorecard** as a team leader.
6. Discover that if you are not **Intentional**, you are not leading.
7. Finally, learn how to **Sustain Success Through Coaching**.

At the end of each chapter you will find a section called *Accelerate Your Leadership.* These are short tips that you can execute *immediately* to accelerate your growth and set yourself up for the next role. I challenge you to work through this after each chapter. Here is the painful reality of life and leadership: We do nothing. We read the magazines, books and blogs. We listen to the TED talks and the conference speakers. And we do nothing. Really, we do nothing.

You are different. Thank you for taking the time and reading this book. I have a special challenge for you. Read the book, be inspired, AND *work* the strategies. As a result, you will grow. Your teams will grow. Your organization will grow. Your influence will grow. You will be promoted (quite possibly more than one level).

When you do this and get promoted, I want to hear your story. Email us at **thisishowirole@renogize.com** and tell us about it. We want to be inspired by you. Who knows? Maybe your story will be included in the next book.

If you haven't noticed, I tend to be direct. This is not because I am a jerk. It is really quite the opposite of that. I care. I care about you. I care about you maximizing your life and your leadership. I care about you impacting others and the world around you. This is what I treasure about being a coach. I work closely with clients for seven to 12 months. They learn and are stretched and challenged and they grow. Everyone around them sees the growth and benefits from the impact. In the end, I do not exist. It is all about them. It is all about you. So with that…

Are you ready to go? Let's start the journey!

This is How I Role

Chapter 1 - Uncover the Human Element

Strategy #1: Uncover the Human Element

AI (Artificial Intelligence) is in the news virtually every day.
Advancement in technology is awesome, and it makes life and business so much more effective and efficient. How far will AI take us? Autonomous vehicles? Robots running factories? Will you someday report to a Bot and not a boss? The technology in our homes is fantastic and scary. Do your "machines" listen in on your conversations? Do you have any privacy? These are all great questions.

I do not know how far it will go, but I do know this: *Humans will never be replaced. Leadership* will never be replaced. No matter how far technology and AI take us, *you* are still needed.

Why is there such a struggle with leadership in organizations today? Quite simply, we have forgotten that we work with humans. *We have forgotten the human element*. If you are ready to be a successful leader who is promoted rapidly, uncover the human element.

Shauna has had a great career and is, what I like to call, "a builder." She is accomplished in building new teams, units and centers at different universities. The key to her success, besides her intellect, is her people skills. She has an innate ability to understand people and meet them where they are. She makes people feel comfortable and want to do well for themselves and for her.

Shauna has learned to tap into the human element. She is open and vulnerable. She shares where she excels and where she struggles. Shauna is not afraid to tell her team about her mistakes and the lessons learned. In response, her team is open and they share their struggles. They view Shauna and the team as a safe place to be imperfect but to always be growing.

This has resulted in a team that will follow her in any circumstance. She is leading them as humans. She has uncovered the human element and her teammates are better people and employees.

Why is uncovering the human element so important?

Hear me out on this... We are all the same. Literally. We are all the same. We are all human. We all feel. We all have emotions. Let's go a bit deeper.

We all feel inadequate. Seriously, we all have a sense of inadequacy. It is born from different circumstances in each of us, but we all have this inner sense.

We all have areas in which we excel. We also all have areas in which we feel weak or inadequate. For example, you could have an engineer with the highest IQ in the world who still feels like he leaves his family wanting more. He might feel like an inadequate spouse or father. A lot of us feel the same way.

You could have a world-class athlete that makes more per at-bat than you make in multiple years. That same athlete has holes in his life and feels inadequate about some things. Do you know how many athletes finish their career completely broke? A *Sports Illustrated* story in 2015 said that 78% of NFL players have gone bankrupt or are under financial distress within five years of retiring. Why? They had skills on the field, but they felt inadequate or were inadequate in handling their money. A lot of us feel the same way.

We all compare ourselves to others. This is a trap. You can always find someone better than you are. You can always find someone worse than you are. *But there is only one you.* If you compare yourself to others and strive to be just like them, you are denying yourself the great gift of being exactly who you were created to be.

Let me show you what I mean. Think of someone you know who has it all together. Typically, this person is someone elevated in your eyes and you minimize yourself in comparison to them. The crazy thing is, that person could be thinking about how you have it all together and that they do not measure up to you. How does that work? That is human nature. Comparisons never work. Be the best you and help others be their best.

We all want to please others. Deep down inside there are others we want to please. In moderation, this is good. I want to please my wife. I want to please my daughter. I want my close friends to be happy with me. I want my clients to be ecstatic about our service and results for them. This is all good.

I also have spent (and wasted) an abundance of my life trying to please everyone. Yes, everyone. It occupied me. If someone was not happy with me, I would try to jump through walls to make things right. Here's the problem. Most of these people did not really care anyway and, no matter what I did, they were not going to be happy with me or anyone else.

So how does this affect us? We spend our time, effort and energy trying to fix something that is not really a problem. Harvard professor of Adult Learning and Professional Development, Dr. Robert Kegan, explains that most people take on a "second job" in an organization. Our first job is what we were hired to do. Our second job is worrying about what others think and how we can make them happy. Kegan goes on to say that if we spend our time doing our first job, we will accomplish more and will eventually realize that our "second job" does not even matter.

At the heart of it, we are human and want others to be happy with us and like us.

We all try to live up to expectations. We put some of these expectations on ourselves (hello, perfectionists). Some expectations are placed on us by others. Some expectations are created in our minds born from the goodness of others.

Let me illustrate this point with a personal story that reveals some of my human element. I grew up in a great Christian home. My parents, my grandparents and my early influencers were all wonderful people who loved me and built me up. As a child I was constantly given praise, "You will do something great." "You will impact thousands of people." "You will make your mark." Phrases like this were common.

Most people may hear this and think that it is great. Why would this be a problem? Though these kind words were meant for my encouragement and my good, I heard something different. I heard that I had to live up to these expectations to keep everyone happy. The praises were heard as expectations that I had to meet in order to be someone. I became preoccupied with meeting these supposed expectations and never told anyone. I did not share it with a single person.

As a result, I slowly began to isolate myself from the reality of what I was feeling inside. As long as I appeared together and made it look like I was meeting expectations, all was well.

Years later I came to a point in my life where I could no longer cover what was happening inside. The appearance and the masks that were covering the real me became too heavy a load to carry. I took the risk of revealing the real me. I shared with my wife first. It was difficult for me to talk about and even more difficult for her to hear. I had not been honest with her about my feelings, pressures and reality of who I was. I shared my true self with some close friends. They gave me support and perspective that shattered a number of the fears dwelling inside of me.

Now that I am a few years removed from wearing a mask, life is incredible. I had a good marriage; now it is a fantastic marriage. I have learned to show incredible grace to others and help them uncover their own humanity. The lessons learned have allowed me to impact many others through personal relationships and coaching. This book is the result of uncovering my own human element.

That is the thing about our humanity. Out of pride, fear, concern, (name your favorite emotion), we hide these human elements. We hide. We put on masks. When you put on a mask, you prohibit yourself from growing. You actually stop the ability of others to impact you because they do not even know the real you. It prohibits you from impacting others. If you are ready to *accelerate your leadership growth and promotability*, you have to expose your humanity. Let others see what is going on inside of you. You also need to pave the way for your people at work to be real and open and share their own humanity.

Are you starting to see it? We are all the same. We are human and as humans we have these thoughts and patterns and concerns.

What we need to do is own the fact that we are human *and* realize that every single person we work with is a human also. We are all the same. Let's own our humanity and *sameness* and make it a driver in how we live and lead. Can you imagine a world with real, vulnerable people? When you uncover the human element in yourself and others, you will be on your way to leadership effectiveness. You will maximize your current role and be preparing for the next role.

You have probably heard the acronym G.O.A.T. It is typically a sports reference that means "Greatest of All Time." If you consider the NFL, do you think this is Tom Brady, Walter Payton or Jim Brown? It is a great debate. In the NBA, is it Wilt Chamberlain, Michael Jordan or LeBron James?

I want to put a spin on this acronym as we discuss leaders. There is one leader that I think stands tallest among them all. I call him The Greatest of All Leaders, or The G.O.A.L. Throughout these pages I will reference The G.O.A.L because in order to be the best, we need to learn from the best.

The G.O.A.L. said that we are all the same. He actually said that the boss is not superior to the direct report (no, not in that exact language but that was the concept). Leaders that have great self-awareness realize that there are different roles people fill, but one is not superior to another. This is the foundation for the concept of servant leadership.

Servant leadership is growing in popularity and effectiveness because it taps into the human element. The G.O.A.L is essentially the founder of this concept.

There is usually a coaching session early on with my clients where this strategy comes out. Uncovering the human element with Wade has changed his life. I began working with Wade because he was struggling in his new role. Wade did a fantastic job as an individual contributor, working in people's homes and installing hardware. Wade was promoted to managing his own field office. He began training new hires by taking them along on his calls and showing them the ropes. His personality shined and people loved working for him. Those he trained were successful themselves. Wade did so well he was promoted to regional manager overseeing thirteen field offices.

Let's Get Real: We Need to Talk about Civility

We live in a culture that is quickly becoming *uncivil*. Think about what is happening in our world today. We have a culture that says it is okay to be two-faced. You can say one thing *and* do the opposite, and you are okay. Or what about the oxymoron of our culture, "I am completely tolerant of all people, as long as they agree with me." Really? When did that become okay?

When we allow incivility in the work place, we create employees who are defensive. Trust is lost. If you are a leader and you do not address incivility, you lose the trust of your best employees. Your passivity empowers those who act in an uncivil manner. Nobody can do his or her best work in these circumstances. It has a negative impact personally and professionally.

- Race is not a reason to treat someone disrespectfully.
- Political party is not a reason to treat someone disrespectfully.
- Gender is not a reason to treat someone disrespectfully.
- Intelligence is not a reason to treat someone disrespectfully.
- Religion is not a reason to treat someone disrespectfully.
- A favorite sports team is not a reason to treat someone disrespectfully.
- Someone treating me disrespectfully is not a reason to treat someone disrespectfully.
- A difference of opinion is not a reason to treat someone disrespectfully.
- (You fill in the blank) _____ is not a reason to treat someone disrespectfully.

This incivility is intolerable. There is no need for it. *Real leaders set the pace in acting, living and leading with civility.* Why? Because we are all human. We are all equal. This is what makes us stand out from the rest of creation.

Former President George W. Bush once said, "Civility is not a tactic or a sentiment. It is the determined choice of trust over cynicism, of community over chaos."

The G.O.A.L. said that we should treat others the way we want to be treated. Do not treat them as they treat you or as though they are less than you. Treat them the same. Do you want civility? Lead with it *first*.

This is where things began to fall apart. The way Wade had always led was not working at this level. As best-selling author, leadership guru and #1 ranked executive coach, Marshall Goldsmith, says, "What got you here will not get you there." A few of the thirteen offices Wade was leading were doing well. He got along with them because the metrics were being met. If metrics were not met, if you were not doing things at maximum capacity, there were problems. Wade would confront them with anger, a raised voice and hostility. He was caught up in managing the process and not leading the people (chapter three covers this concept in detail).

When Wade and I started, he expressed his own concern and did not understand why he was acting this way. We talked about his career and his success. I asked him if he had made mistakes during his tenure at the company. He said yes. I asked Wade if he learned from those mistakes. He said yes, because other leaders helped him understand what he did wrong and how to correct them. Boom. The lightbulb went off for Wade. He was not *leading* his office managers through their mistakes, he was *berating* them for the mistakes. We discussed the human element and the importance of being open and vulnerable. We talked about allowing the fun-loving Wade to come out, even when confronting mistakes. Wade worked hard at making changes, even owning his poor attitude with the field office managers, and apologized to them.

Wade made the adjustments. Ultimately, the positive impact was felt by the field managers, his boss, HR, and even his wife. His boss said that he was amazed by the transformation Wade had made.

As a leader, no matter your role, you need to pave the way for people to see your humanity, and you need to help uncover their humanity.

Do not forget what race you belong to. You belong to the human race. Uncover the human element, and your life will be changed. The lives of those you lead will also be changed.

No matter your role, people will want to follow you....now.

ACCELERATE YOUR LEADERSHIP

- Be real with yourself and identify your humanity.
- Open your eyes to see the humanity of others.
- Have a conversation with your team and uncover their humanity.
- Lead with civility for all people.

This is How I Role

Chapter 2 - Manage Processes. Lead People

Strategy #2: Manage Processes. Lead people.

Ryan works in a manufacturing plant in the mid-west. This location is one of the 19 plants of the corporation. Ryan started working at this plant right out of high school. He knows how to do nearly every job in the plant and he can probably execute each job as well as anyone at the plant.

He is now a director with a number of direct reports. When I first met Ryan, he was quick to share his knowledge of *everything* about the job. I was quite impressed. Coming in with zero knowledge of the industry, he helped me understand their processes and the expected results. I could see that his years of service were a benefit, and that he had immense tribal knowledge.

His company brought me in to help him learn how to lead his team. There had been a mass exodus of those working under him. The company was struggling to identify why someone with so much knowledge and care was unable to keep his team intact. I began to ask Ryan some probing questions about the team, how they worked and how Ryan led them. Ryan provided answers, but he did not answer the questions I was asking. His answers focused on how the team members did not do things correctly. He expressed frustration from having to show them the same thing over and over. He described going to his team members' spots in the plant, moving employees out of the way and telling them he would do it because they were incompetent. Ryan was getting very passionate and animated as he spoke to me, almost angry.

Finally, I interrupted him and thanked him for his answers but addressed the fact that he did not answer my question. He fired back and insisted that he had answered my question. I explained that he told me how he was managing the manufacturing process, but he did not tell me how he was leading the people under him. He looked at me, confused. I explained that manufacturing processes are important, and his team needed to know how to do their jobs, but they also needed someone to *lead them*. It is appropriate to manage processes. That is how we get things done. Simultaneously, we need to lead the people executing the processes because the two things are not the same.

Ryan needed to learn the second strategy of accelerating leadership growth and promotability: *Manage Processes. Lead People.*

Let's take a moment and talk about two common terms in business and life: *manage and lead*. Virtually every organization has managers. Managers are the foundation of many companies. Their role is crucial, and billions of dollars are spent developing the skills of managers.

My preference, however, is to disregard the term *manager*. I like to refer to people who have authority over others as *leaders*, not managers. As I pointed out to Ryan, there is a difference between the two. Processes need to be managed. That is, we need to see that things are done the right way. For example, consider franchise restaurants around the country. They manage the processes and, as a result, are able to provide consistent food, service and atmosphere at thousands of locations around the country. If they did not manage the process, their inconsistency would lead to a loss of business.

On the contrary, people cannot be managed, they need to be led. Yes, people execute the processes, but the people themselves need to be led. They need to be *inspired, empowered* and held *accountable* so that success is shared by all. Processes are rather mechanical in nature and need to be managed. People are people (remember the human element) and therefore deserve to be treated differently. Leadership author, Warren Bennis, coined a phrase that has been used often, "Managers do things right. Leaders do the right things." Doing things right is managing the process. We need to follow protocols and standard operating procedures. Doing the right thing is leadership. This means we might overlook a policy to see that the person we are leading is being put in the best position to succeed.

What happens when you try to manage people? The people being managed will be frustrated. As you watch over them to see that they do things just right (or how *you* would do them) they become paralyzed. They begin to wonder if they can ever do things right. When you manage them, they are seen as a step in the process, a spoke of the wheel, not as a person. They actually feel *manipulated* and *controlled*. This is what happened with Ryan. This is why his team members quit. They left the company, but they *quit* him. Even if you do not want to be controlling or viewed as controlling, people will feel controlled when you try to manage them.

Another negative outcome of managing people when you should be leading them, is that you end up taking responsibility for their work. *Hear me out on this.* If I manage my employees and control every aspect of how they do what they do, I am now responsible for not only the outcome, but also responsible for the actual work they do. On the other hand, if I lead them and set them up for success, they take responsibility for their work and the outcome. As a leader, I need to take ownership of the results as they take responsibility to execute the work. This includes owning the fact that it is my responsibility to set my people up for success, growth and promotability. This is how you role.

Leading your people is always the best approach. Let me illustrate from an interaction that took place during a coaching session last week. I have been meeting with Carter for the past four months. She is an accomplished leader and had been recently promoted to a high position when we began working together.

In a few coaching sessions, she shared her frustration with her project manager. They were not seeing eye-to-eye. Carter felt her project manager, Renee, was not getting the job done and did not show any signs of improvement. The project manager was just as frustrated with how things were going because she wanted to be a great employee and satisfy Carter and the organization.

I asked Carter what she was doing to lead Renee through this difficult season. She mentioned how she had taken different approaches in showing her what needed to be done and how to do it. Carter said she was stepping in *more* (micro-managing) and simultaneously trying to step *back*. Her frustration was very apparent.

In our most recent session, the conversation turned. Carter mentioned that she and Renee saw each other at a company lunch. Normally, Carter would sit with her peers. This time, she decided to sit with her project manager. They had a great conversation and both felt that their personal relationship blossomed. They found some common likes and even dislikes. Both acknowledged that they were frustrated with the result of their efforts and neither wanted it to be that way.

Since the lunch, Carter and Renee have met a few times, and things have been totally different. Renee has offered some great ideas, and Carter has given her the freedom to execute on them.

Renee is now getting the outcomes that Carter and the company expected, because she has the freedom to produce them in her way. Carter has become more open, and she now understands the work style of her project manager.

I asked Carter what changed. She said that once she personally realized who Renee truly is, she sees her as great person with wonderful skills. She trusts her more and understands the human element of her project manager.

Carter is now leading Renee. She is no longer managing the person in the role of project manager. She is leading the person that fills the role of project manager.

We have to lead people. We have to tap into their brilliance. It is our job to set them up for success. How do you know what they need to be successful? Ask them. Seriously, walk up to them and say, "What do you need from me so that I can set you up for success?"

The first time you ask this question, your reports will be stunned and may not have an answer. Ask them to think about it and readdress it at a later time. When they do provide you with an answer, do your best to provide your team members with what they are asking. Common responses are things like more autonomy, clearer expectations, shared accountability, and appreciation for doing a good job.

Another leadership consulting company, Living As A Leader (www.livingasaleader.com), has a definition of leadership that I really like. They say, "Leadership is the balance of accountability and inspiration, getting results through people."

Leadership is about results. Equally important, it is getting those results *through* people. Not in spite of people. Not by manipulating people. Not by parenting people. Not by managing people. But by leading people!

Ryan adapted his behavior and began to lead his team. He sought to understand them and why they did things the way they did. It was a difficult adjustment for him to realize that his way may not be the best way. His team had some great ideas. It may not have increased their speed or effectiveness, but they felt heard, acknowledged and respected. Ryan is still growing and his team is responding in a positive way.

Your people have names. We all owe a debt of gratitude to Gary Portnoy and Judy Hart Angelo for their song, "Where Everybody Knows Your Name," that came to fame through the sitcom, *Cheers*. From 1982 to 1993, you could tune into your TV and hear that great song. Remember these lyrics:

Making your way in the world today,
Takes everything you've got.
Taking a break from all your worries,
Sure would help a lot.

Wouldn't you like to get away?

Sometimes you want to go
Where everybody knows your name,
And they're always glad you came.
You wanna be where you can see,
Our troubles are all the same.
You wanna be where everybody knows
Your name.

Come on, admit it. The tune is in your head now. It will be there for the rest of the day. You are welcome!

If you are unfamiliar with the sitcom, you have missed one of the great examples of the importance of being known and called by your name. *Cheers* featured the lives of some individuals who were "regulars" at a bar with that name. When one character, played by George Wendt, entered the bar, there was a resounding "Norm!" from the patrons. What a sound. The sound of his name.

Did you know that one of sweetest sounds in any language is the sound of your name? You can be in the middle of a crowded, noisy room full of people you do not know, and if someone twenty feet away says your name, you will whip your head around to see who said it! Your ears are tuned in to hear your name. Your emotions are programmed to hear and respond to your name.

Say your name out loud. Seriously. Say it out loud right now. You love the sound of that word. Your name rings beautifully in your ears.

This reality is crucial for you as a leader. What is my point? You need to know the names of your people. You need to say their names out loud and know their stories.

Let's break this song down into some leadership principles.

1. **Making your way in the world today,**
   Takes everything you've got.
   Taking a break from all your worries,
   Sure would help a lot.

The simple truth is that work today is stressful. Most people are called on to do more with less. The pressures of competition, bottom lines, co-workers, and life in general create situations where we often feel helpless. Making your way in the world today *does* take a lot. And yes, we would all like a break from the worries.

As a leader, you cannot always take away people's worries and give them a break. You *can*, however, acknowledge that your people are feeling these pressures. You can honor them for working hard every day. If it has been a stressful week, let them know you are aware of it and tell them, using their names. For example, "Hey George, I know this has been a tough week, and we are all feeling the pressure. Thank you for working hard and standing strong with us. Your contributions are valuable, and they make a difference. You make a difference here, George."

2. **Sometimes you want to go**
   Where everybody knows your name,
   And they're always glad you came.
   You wanna be where you can see,
   Our troubles are all the same.
   You wanna be where everyone knows your name.

Do you see what this chorus teaches?
- We all want people to know our names and be glad we came. When was the last time you praised your people, by name, for showing up? If you have not done that in a while, or ever, go do it. Now. Literally, go do it. It will lift their spirits and yours.
- Let them know that you all are working together, you share in the

struggle and troubles. The work is a *we* thing, not an us-versus-them thing.

- Talk to your people and let them hear their name when things are going well, and not just when something is wrong. Praise them when you use their name.

We all wish we had a bar like Cheers where we could walk in and hear others shout our own name with loud voices. Imagine that place not being a bar, but your place of work. Imagine the joy it would bring to your colleagues. It would be a place where everyone would want to go.

When you are a leader, role and title are irrelevant. A title will not make you or me a leader. Likewise, *not* having a title does not disqualify a person from leading. Stepping up and leading people is what makes a difference. When you do this, you will be noticed. If this is how you role, you will be promoted to have an even larger impact on people.

ACCELERATE YOUR LEADERSHIP

- Think of a time when you managed people unproductively. What did not work for you in this situation?
- Identify the inner brilliance of your co-workers and set them up for success.
- Know the name of every person in your realm of influence and use their name every time you encounter them.

This is How I Role

Chapter 3 - Practice People Whispering

Strategy #3: Practice People Whispering

Cesar Millan has come to fame due to his incredible ability to train dogs. Cesar does not just engage in training any dog, he trains the worst of the bunch. He has an innate ability to understand the dogs and work with them to change the most difficult and aggressive behaviors they exhibit. For this reason, Cesar has been named the Dog Whisperer. Perhaps you have seen the show by the same title.

I am amazed in watching Cesar work with these canines. There are times when I cringe because I just know the dog is going to explode and bite Cesar. Maybe he will lose a finger, an arm or his face! It is riveting television. In the end, due to his observational skills and knowledge of dog behavior, he is able to lead them and their owners to successful and beneficial relationships. Cesar is truly the leader of the pack.

If you are ready to accelerate your leadership growth and be promoted, remember this, *Leadership is influence and influence is behavior.* In the same way that Cesar knows the behavior of dogs, you need to know leadership behaviors. There is an old saying about leadership that suggests if you want to know if you are leader, look behind you. If people are following, you are a leader. If they are not following, you are not a leader. People will not follow what you say; they will follow what you do and how you behave. How you behave is what makes you stand out as a leader.

Over the years, I have been blessed to work with hundreds of leaders from different industries. In all of our engagements we focus on behaviors because leadership is behavior. Sometimes these are bad behaviors. I like the term that Marshall Goldsmith uses for these. He calls them limiting behaviors. They are limiting you from leading well. They are limiting your people from growing, and they are limiting the success of your organization.

When organizations have people attempting to lead with limiting behaviors, those who are being led get frustrated. People become disengaged and expectations are not met. These are the type of leaders that I often coach. The majority have a limiting behavior (or two or three or more) that is holding them back. I come in and work with them over a period of time to help them realize the behaviors, understand the impact of the behaviors, and overcome the behaviors. I have had multiple engagements where the company is at its wits end. They want to help their leader overcome these behaviors, but they do not know how to help them make the shift.

I also want you to know that these leaders have some empowering behaviors that have elevated them to their current position. In our engagements, we also work diligently to maximize these positive behaviors, so their impact is significant.

The majority of our clients have overcome these limiting behaviors and become successful leaders. They deserve the credit for this transformation because they have worked hard to change. Change is difficult enough. When *you* are the one changing, it is even more difficult. My wife, Jen, has heard some of these turn-around stories about our clients, and as a result, has started calling me "The People Whisperer." The great thing is that *all* of the techniques I use to help these leaders change behavior can be used by you too. This is strategy #3 – Practice People Whispering.

Leadership is a privilege; it is not a right. It is a privilege to lead others and to invest in them. It is an honor to know that people are willing to follow you and put their professional success in your hands. This type of trust is a privilege. Treat leadership and followers with the respect it is due.

An old adage states that people do not care how much you know until they know how much you care. To Practice People Whispering, we start by getting to know our people. The first step is what I call a *personal deep dive*. It is a simple process that will take some time. Here is what you do: Arrange a face-to-face appointment with each one of your people, individually, for an hour. Let them know that you want to get to know them and their story. Everyone has a story; get to know theirs. Let them know that what you hear is confidential, unless they want it shared.

This is about *connection*. You need to connect with your people on a personal level if you are going to maximize the business output from them. We were created as relational people who need to connect to others. John Maxwell, a well-known leadership author and speaker, says, "Connecting is the ability to identify with people and relate to them in such a way that it increases our influence with them." People Whispering is a great strategy to find connection points, develop the relationship and influence behavior.

It all starts with a personal deep dive. We ask questions and invite stories by opening lines such as these:

- Tell me about your family when you were growing up.
- How many siblings do you have?
- What did you do in middle school and high school as extra-curricular activities?
- Why did you select your college degree?
- Tell me about your biggest win, professionally.
- Tell me about your biggest disappointment, professionally.
- Tell me about your spouse. Tell me about your kids.
- Come up with some of your own questions....

People will share at different levels based on their personalities and their trust in you. Some will share more details than you want. Others will just gloss the surface. Either is perfectly fine—do not force anything.

As they are sharing, you need to note to yourself the areas in which you have some commonality. It may be one tiny thing they share, but you can find it. Taking written notes during this time is not seen as a negative. It shows you are interested, fully present and engaged.

During the same meeting and after they share, you *must* share some things about yourself. You may not have the time to go as deeply as they have, but the conversation must be reciprocal because leadership is executed in relationship! It is a two-way street, so you must share also.

Leaders often feel this puts them in a vulnerable position because an employee can use personal knowledge against them. Some leaders feel that this shows them as weak, so they do not want to be open or share anything about themselves. If this is your fear, you are probably leading from a place of positional leadership. Positional leadership says, "I am your boss because the hierarchy chart says so." We are not talking about being a boss. We are talking about being a leader. There is a huge difference between bossing from a position in a hierarchy and leading by influence.

I understand your concern about sharing your life with others at work. An employee may go and talk about what he or she heard. Understand this: If you are telling all of your team members these things in one-on-one sessions, you control what is known. If an employee goes out to talk to the team about what you have shared, they have already heard directly from you and therefore it has no negative impact.

Let's be honest here. You have reasons or excuses to not be open and share. Leaders overcome these perceived barriers and do what is right anyway.

Back to the process…

When you find commonality in your stories, make it known. Give that nugget of information and similarity extreme focus. If you were born in the same state, make it known. If you went to college against a rival of their college, have some friendly banter about each school's sport teams. If you both have three siblings, let it guide your connection. You get it. Make the connection.

When your colleagues and direct reports feel known by you, and they know you, they will begin to follow you. Now that you know more about them, you can begin to tap into their brilliance and lead them to heights they have never known. That is the power of connection. That is the power of People Whispering.

People Whispering allows you to connect on a deep level rapidly. This quick connection paves the way for accelerated growth.

Erin was like so many leaders today. She moved up the ladder quickly, probably too fast. She had the technical skills and knew how to do the job well, but as a leader she was facing extreme pushback. Members of her department were not happy, and many had left.

I spent two days at Erin's place of work to interview a number of people in her department. Her team shared some true limiting behaviors with me. They described her in the following ways: She is aloof. She does not care. She is preoccupied. She seems more interested in her own things and not us. She is always mad at us. We only see her when something is wrong. She executes with the mentality of command and control!

When Erin and I sat down together to talk, she was somewhat stiff and skeptical of my presence. She was consumed with wondering what her colleagues had said. After some pleasantries, I let her know that I was there for her, and I wanted her to succeed. I also let her know our conversation was confidential and that I would be sharing with her some of the perceptions of her team. We dove in, and I began to ask her the questions of the personal deep dive.

With each opening question or statement, Erin began to roll out her story. She shared some interesting insights from her childhood and growing up. She began to relax and smile some as she shared. I took notes and listened actively with genuine interest in her and her life story. She continued on and shared some tough experiences she had faced. She opened up about some major life issues that were impacting her at that very moment. There was a lot of emotion in her voice. Though Erin needed to work on some limiting behaviors, I began to understand *why* she was doing some of the things she was doing.

By the time the personal deep dive was over, I felt like I knew her, and more importantly, she felt known. Just sharing her story brought her some peace. She also got to know me a bit because a relationship needs to go both directions. Where there is relationship, there is trust. Erin now had a trust in me, and we were able to begin navigating some difficult feedback and perceptions from others.

Over the course of our six months together, Erin grew tremendously. She worked with her colleagues and their perceptions of her changed as her behaviors changed. She learned how to be open and real with me and her colleagues. She shared her new knowledge of limiting behaviors with her team. Erin said that she was sorry for the negative impact she had on them. This was a huge step for her and can be a huge step for you too. Two of the most difficult words in the English language are, "I'm sorry." They are difficult to say, but they are transforming. When you say "I'm sorry," you open the door to forgiveness and growth. Erin did this and it changed her leadership.

I have been through this deep dive exercise over a hundred times now. The coaches that work with me have been through this exercise. It has yet to fail! It always creates a bond and trust that allows us to move forward and deal with reality in a powerful way. It shows these leaders the power of being real and sharing their story.

Why is People Whispering so powerful? Each of us have an inner longing for relationship. We all have a need to be known. The G.O.A.L had numerous occasions during his time leading where he addressed the person, not the problem. He called people by name. He had sympathy and empathy with their plight because he took the time to listen and notice. He was painfully honest with people about their limiting behaviors. He encouraged them to stop those behaviors. The result was thousands of changed lives. He led with relationship.

To be the best leader you can be—the type of leader that others follow and gets promoted—you need to be a people whisperer.

The G.O.A.L.

If you are trying to figure out who The G.O.A.L. is, let me go ahead and tell you. It is my opinion that the Greatest Of All Leaders is Jesus. You can debate this, but in my view, this is the case. Whether you agree or not is fine. Your faith background or belief system does not matter. We can still learn from great leaders. Jesus was real and did walk this earth and shared incredible leadership lessons with us. That is why I lay some of them out in this book.

Let me give you a few examples of how People Whispering changes things.

During a coaching session with Bob, he expressed his concerns about making mistakes and being fired. His preoccupation with these thoughts and feelings was holding back his execution. The odd thing about Bob's feelings is that he was viewed as an all-star leader. People loved him at work, and he was being prepped for an executive role. His company brought me in to help accelerate his development so he would be ready for that promotion quickly. Bob's view of himself and his concerns of being fired did not mesh with how others viewed him.

Bob and I had been through the personal deep dive together. He had shared that his dad had been fired, without cause, on three different occasions. This history with his father was impacting Bob's thoughts today. Knowing this history, I was able to help Bob see that, even though his story about his father was real, his fears in his current job were not justified. This gave him peace and, over time, he has been able to let those fears subside. Had I not *known* Bob and this part of his life, I never would have been able to help him connect the dots and move forward.

During my personal deep dive with Kerry, I learned she had quite an eventful childhood. She spent a number of her formative years in the Middle East because her dad worked for a company there. This international experience accelerated her learning in a number of areas. She went back and forth from the U.S. and overseas a few times. When she entered high school, she came back to the U.S. without her parents and attended boarding school. She did not care much for the first school and went to another one the next year in a different state. She was a great student and excelled in these situations.

This history made Kerry a very strong and independent person. In her current job, there are some issues because her team and the other teams in the organization feel that Kerry does not share information very well. They feel she makes decisions independent of their feedback and rarely shares the rationale for her decisions. This was causing friction, and her colleagues were not seeing her as a team player. Since I knew her from the personal deep dive, I was able to understand why she was behaving this way. There was nothing nefarious in her; she was just used to making her own decisions and being confident in them. I was able to help her connect the dots of her history and how her habits of independence were a negative in a team environment. Her awareness of this has had a profound effect on her. She is now working to overcome these limiting behaviors. If I did not know Kerry's story, I could not have helped her make this breakthrough.

Cesar Milan is not a great success because he knows how to understand dogs. Yes, his ability as the dog whisperer is the foundation of his success, but there is more to it. It is one thing to understand dogs and why they do what they do. Cesar is successful because he is able to take the information about the dogs, find ways to correct negative behaviors, and teach the dog new behaviors. However, even this is not the key to his success.

The key to his success is the ability to teach dog owners what he sees and help them connect the dots. He teaches them how to lead the dog to success. This is what sets Cesar apart. If he could not teach others to do what he does, he would not have a sustainable business. He cannot be with the dog 24/7, but the dog owner (leader) can be.

If you are ready to excel as a leader and be promoted, you need to use the strategy of People Whispering. You not only need to use it, but you also need to let your team know what you are doing. Let them see the benefits of knowing one another.

I use the strategy of *People Whispering* with my clients every single time. I also work diligently to let them know what I am doing, why I am doing it and how they can do it to impact others.

Knowing how to use a strategy as a leader is crucial. Being able to teach that strategy to your people will set you apart. There is a misconception that if I share my "secrets" of leadership success with others, I will no longer be valuable. This is a myth! Share your secrets. Set others up for success. The people around you will be grateful for it, and you will have the opportunity to impact more and more people because of it.

So far, we have *Uncovered the Human Element.* We have learned that we need to *Manage Processes, Lead People.* We have seen the benefits of *Practicing People Whispering.* These three strategies are really about you and how you lead. They are strategies that elevate you individually and accelerate your career. Now we need to change our focus a bit. Twenty-first century business is being executed in teams. We must focus on how we lead teams and impact others in groups.

Are you ready? First, work through the items on the next page, and then ROLE ON to the next chapter.

ACCELERATE YOUR LEADERSHIP

- Have a personal deep dive with your direct reports.
- Identify and connect the dots of why they do what they do.
- Lead them in their own unique way.
- Teach someone else the strategy of People Whispering.

This is How I Role

Chapter 4 - Win with T.E.A.M.

Strategy #4: Win with T.E.A.M.

I am a sports fan. I realize that not everyone loves sports, but I do, and it shines through in a number of ways. There are great lessons about life and leadership that we can learn from sports.

For years, people have debated which sports are better. Are individual sports such as golf, tennis or bowling best? (Yes, I know that these have doubles and team options, but they are individual sports.) Or are team sports such as football and basketball best?

In business today, you typically do not have an option; you are a part of a team. As a leader, you are both leading a team *and* are a member of a team. This reality is only going to grow in the coming years; it will not diminish. That is why it is crucial we discuss working on teams.

There are some incredible books about working on teams. I am a fan of the work of Patrick Lencioni, who does a masterful job describing the ins and outs of teamwork in a professional setting. *The Five Dysfunctions of a Team* and *The Ideal Team Player* are some of his most popular and powerful works.

Our company, Renogize Professional Coaching, has had a number of opportunities to work with teams over the years. You will read about some of those opportunities in this chapter. Every good team has the right balance of four key components: trust, energy, accountability and mission. This is our view of T.E.A.M, and the fourth strategy to accelerate your leadership growth and promotability.

It is not uncommon for leaders to complain about their teams. Especially when a leader inherits a team, he or she often complains and laments, "If only I could pick my own team." I understand the sentiment, but do not accept the implied excuse. No matter the hand you are dealt, it is your job as a leader to develop and maximize your team.

Whether you are fixing a dysfunctional team, drafting a new team, or moving a team from good to great, following this strategy will work.

TRUST

Trust is the foundation of any team. Here is what it looked like with one client.

We were called in to work with an executive team of seven people from a company in the public sector. Jim, the CEO, was new to the organization and was growing frustrated with what he saw in his team. Like most organizations, this one was highly siloed. Rather than working together, the leaders wanted the autonomy to run their own divisions without interruption or input; however, they also wanted to tell the other division leaders how to do their jobs. The leaders talked behind one another's backs. They had a tendency to have the "meeting after the meeting" where they shared their dislike for one another.

One of the first things we did was execute an assessment to rate how the executive team members worked together. Trust was rated incredibly low. When we gathered for a two-day off site workshop, we began with this issue of trust. Before we started, I warned the group that we were going to rip the band-aid off some things and that it would not be pretty. I also reassured them that we would work through the issues and show respect for one another in the process.

The team was quick to acknowledge that they did not trust one another. This was good. So many times, we are not honest and just say that everything is good without acknowledging flaws and weaknesses.

These executives owned the fact that they did not trust one another. Their assessment report confirmed this in glaring red ink.

I opened our time together by asking a simple question: "Is trust earned or given?" There were a variety of responses to this question. There is a correct answer. *If you want to be a leader that is impacting others, influencing others and making a difference, you have to extend trust to people from the moment you meet them.*

In his podcasts and written content, social media marketing expert, Gary Vaynerchuk, says that you have to trust early. When you trust early, you pave the way for people to excel.

Remember Strategy #1, The Human Element. We are all human and we are all the same. Because of this, I give you my trust from the start; you don't have to earn it. You may do things to lose my trust over time, but you have my trust from the beginning. It is yours from the beginning because you deserve that trust as a human.

As Jim and the executive team started talking through trust issues, we began to see some common causes of their mistrust.

- They did not see their teammates as being subject matter experts in their field.
- They did not understand the scope of work being done by their teammates.
- They did not know how their work impacted everyone (both good and bad).
- They were working from a mindset that trust is earned, not given.
- They were influenced by gossip and rarely checked to verify the truth (at least that is what I heard from someone else).

Fill in the blanks yourself. What do you see as causes of mistrust on teams?

This team was laying everything out on the table. The conversation itself was actually therapeutic and helped them to begin seeing how they, individually, caused some of the mistrust on the team. Before we moved on from the topic that day, I had the participants go around the table and address each of their executive teammates.

Their task was to express trust and confidence in their teammates' abilities to do their respective jobs. They had to express a commitment to trust their peers to execute. We did not resolve all the executive team's trust issues that day. But we did lay the groundwork to develop the trust necessary to execute.

Trust is built through relationship. This is why we start by uncovering the human element in everyone. This is how people whispering begins to transform surface relationships into substantial relationships where trust is a common result.

Trust is the foundation of effective teams. What can you do right now to develop the trust of your team(s)?

ENERGY

The concept of energy flowing from the leader of a team may be new for you. We are looking at energy from two lenses here. One is the energy you bring you to your team. The other is the energy you expend as the team leader.

First, as the leader (and you are one), your team will respond to the energy you bring to the office every day. Most team leaders think that their team needs to bring the energy. They are the ones that do the work. They need to meet the deadlines and execute so the energy is on them. Wrong! As the leader, you set the tone with your energy.

Hear me out on this. How you show up to work has a direct impact on how your team works. If you show up each morning as though you couldn't care less to be there, your team will work with that same mentality. If you show up to work with a positive attitude, your team will work with a positive attitude and produce at a higher level. You may not think you have this type of influence, but you do. Leadership is influence. Leadership *energy* is influence.

Jim had a few limiting behaviors that were sucking the energy from his team. He had been brought in by the board so that there would be new and fresh ideas. His predecessor had served a number of years on the job, and the organization had become stale. The board selected Jim because he was intuitive and could identify areas that needed improving and help find solutions.

This strength was also a weakness. He identified the issues, but when he shared them, he would express how poorly the previous CEO had done. Jim would lament why the current executives had not done more. He thought the leaders throughout the city were patting themselves on the back but not executing. He was not shy in sharing his impression of *their* city. Jim was not open to the fact that this was now his company in this city and his view needed to change.

You can guess the result. It quickly grew to a point where Jim's team members did not hear *what* Jim said because of *how* he said it. Even in my one-on-one coaching sessions with him, Jim would share these negative ideas. It came to a point when I told him to stop. Stop saying these things. I told him that I did not want to hear him mention the previous CEO again, and I did not want to hear anything bad about the city again. I also did not want him to say it anywhere at anytime again. He agreed! He finally realized how his energy was having a negative impact on the team, his organization and even himself.

Secondly, you need to consider the energy you expend as the team leader. Many leaders feel that their role is to lead the team, and it is the team's job to get stuff done. On the surface, this is accurate. However, when you dig into it, this is not accurate.

Remember Strategy #2, Manage processes. Lead people. If you buy into the concept that your team expends the energy, and you oversee them doing that, you are missing the point. As a leader, you lead the team, and this takes incredible effort and energy.

Consider an orchestra. An orchestra is a collection of brilliant musicians from all different fields (instruments). During a concert, they work diligently to be in sync (like a team) to produce music that drives the emotions of the listener. The musicians are doing all the work. Wait, is that true? *No.*

The next time you attend an orchestra concert, do not just listen to the music; also watch the conductor. She is standing with her back to everyone in the audience (this demonstrates humility as the concert is not about her). She is waving her baton in perfect rhythm to see that each instrument section is executing when it is supposed to. She is conducting the orchestra. Most conductors work up a sweat. It is a full-body experience for them, and every muscle they have is used throughout the performance. The musicians are the ones working, but the conductor exudes more energy than they do to get the job done *together*.

It is the same for a team leader. The team members are doing the work, but you need to work just as hard, if not harder, to keep them in sync. The results represent what you were able to lead the team to accomplish.

During one of our sessions, Jim shared some of his frustration with the number of conversations he needed to have with the executive team for them to execute their roles. He trusted them as the subject matter experts and couldn't understand why they couldn't simply execute and get things done. I explained to Jim, that as the leader, his role is to have these conversations. His responsibility is to communicate, over and over, so that the team is aligned and has clear understanding of what is expected.

It is not Jim's job to expend energy doing the work; his job is to expend energy leading the team to do the work. This work is as exhausting as the work itself.

Having a title does not remove you from having to work hard. As a leader, you need to bring the energy.

ACCOUNTABILITY

Once a team has established trust and everyone, including the leader, is bringing the energy, we can begin to execute. Teams are put together to get things done. Business succeeds because we get things done.

So, how do we get things done as a team? We hold one another accountable. It sounds simple, but it is not easy. Whether you are the team leader or a member, you need to understand accountability. How do we do this?

1. **Own your part.**

   Too often when things are not going well, we look to others and point the finger. We fall into the blame game. There may be members of the team that did not get things done. You need to ask yourself first, did I do everything I could do to help this situation? What could I have done differently? What can I change?

   When you look to yourself first, you find solutions, not problems. For accountability to rise on your team, you must hold yourself accountable first. For some great reading about this I recommend you get *Extreme Ownership* by Jocko Willink and Leif Babin. This book will change your thinking on this topic.

2. **See the big picture.**

   Once you own your part and hold yourself accountable, you can begin to look at the big picture and identify why things are not getting done. Do the team members have a clear picture of their *individual* responsibilities? Do they all know the order things need to be done so they can move the project along? Are the expectations crystal clear?

3. **Be the solution.**

   When you see members of the team struggling or holding the rest of the team back, you have to address it. The longer you wait, the more harm there is to the project and the team. Teams that have established trust and are bringing energy actually become self-policing. They want the project to succeed. They want one another to succeed. As the leader, you need to bring a "can do" attitude and be a part of the solution!

It seems as if leaders fall on two extremes in this area of accountability. They are either really forceful and hold others accountable in a way that drives people out, or they are afraid to hold others accountable. They fear the team members may leave. They are concerned it may hurt someone's feelings. We need to find an effective middle ground on this.

To overcome being forceful, remember the human element and be
sure you are doing your part to set the team up for success. In reference
to being too kind, there is usually an underlying sense of wanting to be
liked. Catch this: If you want to be liked by everyone, you will never be
an effective leader. It is not a question of whether they like you. It is a
question of whether they respect you, the team members and your ability
to lead.

The definition of leadership we shared earlier comes out here. Find
the balance of accountability and inspiration, and you will lead others
successfully.

The G.O.A.L had a team of twelve. He spent significant time investing
in them and developing them so that they could lead others successfully.
On a number of occasions, he struggled because his team was not
grasping his message. He had told them how to do things. He showed
them how to do things. They still messed up. He was frustrated, but he
never gave up. He told them what was wrong (held them accountable)
and continued to give them opportunity (inspiration). In the end, he
stepped away and they did their part to accomplish the mission.

MISSION

For a team to be successful, team members have to know the mission.
What is it that we are trying to accomplish? This could be a short-term
project team or an intact executive team. No matter the team, the
mission is crucial.

In our work with teams, we have found that there are two missions that
are at play simultaneously. As a leader you need to be aware of both and
honor both. There is the team mission and the personal mission.

First, Team Mission

Each team member needs to know what our desired outcome is. *Why*
are we together? What are we here to accomplish?

The *why* is everything and it is usually the piece that gets the smallest
amount of attention. As a leader, you need to let your team members

know how they are doing, and if they are on target. When you do not tell the *why*, they miss the significance of their work. Many experts say that you need to share something seven times in seven different ways before people understand why they are doing something.

Jim came to his executive team with the idea of giving every employee an end-of-year bonus. The organization had a good year, and this would be a small way to show they appreciated the work from everyone. When he brought this idea up to the team, they pushed back on him. Their reaction caught him off guard.

We then discussed how he brought the idea up to the team. His communication with them had been short and sweet. He figured they would all *get it* and want to give the bonuses. What he did not share with them was that the bonuses were a representation of the culture he wanted them to work as a team to create. They had discussed building a culture of service and servant leadership. They agreed that they wanted to be a place where people wanted to come to work. In Jim's eyes, this bonus represented the best of what they wanted to be. He never, however, told the team his reasoning! The *why* makes all the difference.

Once we have the *why*, the *what* makes sense, and the team is able to execute. They all need to buy-in to the team mission. As the leader, you need to be sure they know it.

Second, Personal Mission

As a team leader, you need to acknowledge how your personal mission plays out with the team mission. If the team succeeds, you succeed. If the company gets a profit windfall from the work your team executes, you get promoted. Even though there is no *I* in team, your team is a group of *I*'s who need to be acknowledged.

While leading your team, you need to help them see that team success is their success. The benefit of teams is that you serve multiple roles and learn from those roles. Some days you will lead the team. Other days you may be a follower. One day you are a creator. Another day you are cleaning up messes.

This is how I role! This is part of the concept. No matter the role I play today, I can influence others and grow. As a leader at work, I can grow. As a follower at work, I can grow. As a teammate at work, I can grow. As a parent, sibling, child, friend, my mission is to grow.

When you help others see that your team goal will help them move down the path to their personal goals, everyone wins.

This formula looks simple, but it is not easy. If you truly want to accelerate your leadership growth and promotability, you need to realize that T.E.A.M. is an essential part of the journey. Are you ready to take the next step in your journey? Follow the steps below and ROLE ON.

TRUST

ENERGY

ACCOUNTABILITY

MISSION

ACCELERATE YOUR LEADERSHIP

- Give trust to where you have been holding it back.
- Identify three things that need your energy now.
- Be accountable to your team.
- Hold your team accountable.
- Recite the mission of the team.
- Recite your personal mission.

This is How I Role

Chapter 5 - Learn the New Scorecard

Strategy #5: Learn the New Scorecard

Now that we have covered four of our strategies, this is a good time to take a quick look at where we have been. A key to leadership is remembering the small things and keeping them in the forefront of our minds.

Strategy #1: Uncover the Human Element. We need to be mindful of our humanity and the humanity of our colleagues. We are all the same. We all have feelings of inadequacy and the need to measure up. Because we are the same, let's give one another some grace and work effectively.

Strategy #2: Manage Processes. Lead People. As we go about our work every day, we need to manage the processes or how we do things. We cannot manage people, we need to lead them. If you try to manage them, it will seem like you are putting your thumb on them and holding back the best they have to offer. When you lead your team members, you are removing barriers and setting them up for success.

Strategy #3: Practice People Whispering. As leaders, we need to develop a connection with our people. Do a personal deep dive and get to know who they are, how they operate and how you can maximize their impact. As the leader, you need to be open and vulnerable with them. People will follow you when they know you.

Strategy #4: Win with T.E.A.M. Business is accomplished in teams today. As the leader, you need to be prepared to take your team(s) to the next level. You do this by establishing a baseline of trust and bringing the energy every day to push your team forward. When you lead effectively, the team will hold themselves accountable to accomplish the task. Finally, you keep them all focused on the mission. This is the team mission and their personal missions.

I hope you are feeling good right now. I know you have been implementing some of the acceleration ideas at the end of the chapters. It is making a difference. Your coworkers are beginning to appreciate the differences in how you are leading. Let's continue to Role On.

Strategy #5: Learn the New Scorecard

Tory was a brilliant scientist with some pretty solid people skills. This combination led him to a new opportunity to work at a top university as a department chair. This was his first time serving as a chair, and he was excited about the opportunities it would create.

I was brought in to coach Tory in this new role. The dean of his school wanted me to help this scientist get plugged in quickly to make an impact. The dean also knew that this was Tory's first time with direct reports, and the skills Tory needed for success would be different than those needed in past roles. He would now have to achieve results through others.

Tory and I hit it off from the beginning on a personal level. The personal deep dive (people whispering) allowed us to move our relationship beyond the surface and deal with real issues immediately. The engagement was going really well. Tony was coachable and excited about the variety of work in the department. He was doing such a good job that the faculty in his department were becoming more engaged and producing research at a higher level. Tory was able to obtain a huge grant that was expected to propel the department forward. Things were great. Success. End of story.

Not so fast. Whether dealing with success or difficulties, there are hurdles to be overcome. The biggest hurdle for Tory was not about how to execute or how to produce great research. His hurdle was a mental one common to every individual that makes the transition from individual contributor to leader. It involves a shift in focus. If Tory could jump and clear this hurdle, he and his department would be a great success. If not, it would hold them all back. The same is true for you. Let me use a sports analogy to explain.

As a sports fan, I have occasionally had the opportunity to talk with people who do not share my enthusiasm. This does not bother me. I usually try to find something the other person is interested in and make that the focus of our time. There are times, however, when people try to hide their lack of interest and speak as if they understand sports when they do not. What is the result? You might be at a baseball game, the batter hits a home run and the person next to you screams, "Touchdown!" I smile as I bury my face in my hands. I appreciate the attempt, but it falls flat.

Here is the thing. If you do not know what sport you are playing, it is difficult to know the score. When you move from being an individual contributor (with no direct reports) and are promoted to a leader (with one or more direct reports) the game changes. It becomes a totally different game. A problem arises when new leaders try to use the same scorecard even though they are playing a new game.

Let me illustrate my point. When you are an individual contributor at a company or university, your scorecard, or metrics or things that are tracked may be any of the following:

- Your number of sales
- Your total sales volume for the month
- Your new innovations/inventions
- Your research project
- Your grant money
- Your publishing
- Your websites designed
- Your documents reviewed
- Your number of satisfied customers
- Your positive customer reviews

I think you get the point. These are all great metrics, and they make a beautiful scorecard by which you can assess your effectiveness. Do you notice something about this scorecard? The first three letters of every item is *you*. These are all individual accomplishments because you are an individual contributor.

Because you hit it out of the ballpark as an individual contributor, you were promoted to lead others. The game changed, but no one explained the new game or the new scorecard.

Newsflash: the game is not about *you* anymore. I know, that is tough to swallow. Read it again and experience the pain of it all. Now read it out loud. Hear yourself say those words. Let's personalize it and say it out loud: (say your name), it is not about you anymore.

It is now about *them*. Your team. Your direct reports.

To be a good leader, you need to realize this change. To be a great leader that influences others and gets promoted again and again, you need to master this change.

Tory had a breakthrough about midway through our seven-month engagement together. We were talking, and he was very down emotionally. I asked him why he was feeling that way, and he could not put his finger on it. Things were going well. His team was happy and executing. His dean was happy with the department and the impact they were having on the school. Everything looked good.

As Tory went on, he began explaining that he did not have as much time for his own research. The time he spent leading had taken away from his time to be doing his own work. His team and department were being viewed as successful, but personally Tory felt he was failing because he did not have anything to show for *his* work. I understood his sentiment and acknowledged his pain. I also let him know that as a leader, he was being viewed differently. He was seen as effective and engaging, and his team was performing at a higher level. That day we began to explore what the new scorecard looked like for him. It is a scorecard of what *we* have done together. Have *we* met *our* goals? How has the *team* done?

The human element makes this difficult. This transition feeds into the thoughts of inadequacy we all share. Up until now, we have been praised for what we have accomplished as individuals. That is no longer the case. It is about the team, not us. It can make us feel inadequate or unnecessary. That is understandable. In reality, it empowers the human element. As you invest in the team's success, they feel valued and important. They will be engaged and produce at a higher level. That is the human response. You will also feel validated and realize that you are impacting them personally and professionally.

Being a great leader and moving to a new scorecard takes humility. In fact, humility is one of the defining characteristics of great leaders. I want to be sure we are on the same page here, so let's define humility. Most people think that humility is thinking less of themselves. That is not humility. That is self-deprecation. Humility is not thinking less of yourself; it is thinking of yourself less often. It means that you consider your colleagues first.

Tory, and you, will be viewed as great leaders when you get high marks on the new scorecard. Here is a small sampling of what this card might include:

- **Setting people up for success.** As a leader, your role is to see that your team members have everything they need to succeed. Ask them for help in determining what these things may be. This will be different based on the style and personalities of your team members. Be diligent in providing all that they need for success.

- **Motivating for excellence.** See that you are in tune with what motivates your people and be sure to supply it for them. How do you know what motivates them? You may already know from your personal deep dive. Simply ask each individual, "What motivates you to work hard and with excellence?"

When we think of motivation, we usually consider tangible rewards like a bonus, a raise or additional time off. These things help, but they are not lasting. You need to find the intrinsic motivation. What is it that makes each of your team members want to get up in the morning and come to work? What engages them or elevates their game? Find those answers and you will be developing a team of all-stars.

- **Leading to their style.** Ineffective leaders think that their teams need to adjust to them. Highly effective leaders adjust their style to every individual they lead. This takes work and practice, but it is life changing. If you are leading an introvert, do not ask that person for responses in public situations. When leading someone who is determined and likes to move fast, do not put him or her behind a desk with nothing to do or monotonous routine work. I highly recommend you use some form of assessment to understand the working style of your people and adjust to what each needs. MBTI, DISC or Strength Finders are all great assessments that will give you a picture of your people as individuals.

Of course, to lead to the styles of others, you first need to know *your* style. You need to take these assessments too. Leadership begins with self-awareness. Begin by exploring your style. Then, as you learn the styles of others, you will see where your style provides them with encouragement, and you will see where your style drives them crazy. Yes, I know it is hard to believe, but not everyone thinks your style is the greatest. Learn your team members' styles, adjust to them and watch the productivity increase.

- **Delegating and empowering.** Effective leaders give their team members important tasks that will stretch them and explain *why* they are giving them the task. You don't delegate just to take a task off your plate. You delegate because you've identified the right person who possesses the right key trait. The *why* is everything. When you explain the why, you are setting a person up for success, and the knowledge will motivate that person to achieve. The why is specific to the individual because you know that person's style and are capitalizing on that knowledge. Then, give the person the power and authority to execute. Do not look over his or her shoulder. Do not pretend that you have given the individual the task. Truly hand it off and let the person execute.

- **Developing your successor.** As a leader, you want to work yourself out of a job. When you invest in one or more people to take your place, everyone wins. This is foreign to many of us. If you identify one or two people as your successors, and you invest in them, it will move you to a place of leading rather than doing. You will teach the finer details of your role. It will remind *you* why you do things certain ways and why these methods work (or don't work). When you develop your successor and work yourself out of a job, you do not lose your job. You pave the way for your company to elevate you to a higher position.

- **Providing developmental feedback.** Too many leaders spend their time telling people what they are *not* doing right. It is time to change this. Yes, they need to know areas to improve, and they do need feedback. I like the term that Marshall Goldsmith has for this—*feedforward.* Instead of telling your people what they are doing wrong, tell them what they can do differently to execute at higher level. Have you tried doing it this way? Have you considered this approach? This pushes your team members forward; it does not beat them up for the past. Once you've shared ways to improve, your team members can go out and try a new method or approach. You can then debrief with them about how that went. Through this open dialogue and communication, you are both learning how to be effective on the job and in communicating.

- **Giving praise and recognition.** Let your team members know they are doing a good job. Do not be patronizing with it, be specific. "You did this really well and it impacted all of us in a positive way." A popular phrase is "what gets rewarded gets repeated." If you want people to repeat some great work, reward it when it happens, and it will continue to happen. I have heard warnings from plenty of leaders suggesting that if you praise your people they will think "they have arrived" and do not need to work hard anymore. Or, they will want a raise or a promotion because you have praised them. This may happen occasionally, but it will not be the norm.

  Catch this: as a leader, you need to do what is right for people. If they twist it into something it is not, that is on them. The vast majority will appreciate your praise and recognition and work harder. Do not be stopped by the minority, do what is right for the majority. I want to praise you, in advance, for giving reward and recognition to your people.

- **What would you add to this list?**

It is difficult to make the mental leap from individual contributor to leader because it is counterintuitive. We think that in order to move up in an organization or life, we need to tell people what *we* are doing. This makes sense but it is not the reality of the situation.

Consider it from this angle. We think that we need to get our names out to be noticed if we are going to move up and have opportunities (the old scorecard). Look at it from the perspective of the executives or the board at your company. If your team is doing an incredible job, meeting metrics and influencing the organization, they will be noticed. There may be some all-stars on your team that are honored and stand out. People will notice them. Simultaneously, without you tooting your own horn, they will be noticing who led the all-stars to success.

The G.O.A.L. is the greatest leader of all time. We know a number of things that he was able to accomplish. We also know about his team. We know how they worked, how they impacted others and how they led a revolution that still ripples through our lives today. He developed his twelve and sent them out to be the face of the revolution. He actually stepped out of the picture entirely and let them be seen as the leaders. Did we forget about him? No. That is part of why he is the greatest leader of all time.

We know the names of great head coaches in sports today—and they do not even play the game. They are known because of their ability to pull the best out of their teams. We have heard the names of CEOs from the largest companies in the world. They have thousands of employees that are working diligently every day. Many of those employees know more about how to do what the company does than the CEO. The employees are the reason for the success. These CEOs praise their employees. Yet, you still know the CEO's name. Do not worry about your efforts as a leader going unnoticed.

Learn the new scorecard. Make the mental transition and realize that your team's success *is* your success. Tory is still in the process of making the change. He has come a long way, but he has a way to go. Because he has acknowledged the need to change and is working through it, Tory is winning.

Leadership is not easy. It takes work to be effective as a leader. You have to be intentional in what you do or it will not happen. That is where we are going with strategy #6. Let's ROLE ON.

Let's Get Real About Difficult Conversations

To be an exceptional leader, you need to have difficult conversations. These can be about conflict scenarios, lack of performance, attendance issues or limiting behaviors. The list is endless, and the opportunities for the conversations are plentiful.

Why do we avoid difficult conversations? Because they are difficult! Truthfully, if you enjoyed such conversations, you would come across as a jerk. When you avoid them, difficult issues become crippling situations.

When you have executed the five strategies we have discussed so far, these conversations become more bearable. In addition, you need to have a plan for your difficult conversations.

Here are a few steps to make these difficult conversations *powerful* conversations.

1. Share only what you have observed. Do not pass judgment or use condemning language. Simply share what you have observed and why that behavior is causing problems.
2. Seek their input and make it a conversation. After you have shared your observations, allow the other person to give a response. Sometimes that person will be full of excuses. Sometimes you will learn something that explains the entire situation.
3. Design a plan for next steps. If all we do is discuss the behavior and say, "Stop it," we will leave the conversation with no change. Map out what you expect to be different and let your team member explain what he or she will do differently.
4. Follow up on the conversation. If you do not follow up at a later time, you will not move the marker on the behavior.

5. As a humble leader that is investing in people, you will never be joyful in these conversations. With experience and good results, you will grow to realize that they are vital, and they will set you apart as a leader.

ACCELERATE YOUR LEADERSHIP

- Identify if you are playing with the correct scorecard.
- Determine what elements need to be included on your new scorecard.
- Have that difficult conversation you have been putting off for months. Do it today.
- Exercise "Feedforward" today.

This is How I Role

Chapter 6 - Lead with Intention

Strategy #6: Lead with Intention

During a recent coaching call, my client, Michelle, was sharing how her team meeting went that day. During her team meeting, Michelle had said, "We need to be intentional about this." Her teammate, whom I had formerly coached over a year ago, shot back at her, "That's from Sean. He is *so* your coach. That is something he would say." They both got a good laugh out of it (at my expense). It provided them the opportunity to share with their team what intentional leadership is all about. Catch the importance of this. I am intentional in making my clients intentional. They know it. They hear it. They recognize it. That is intentionality.

Though this strategy seems obvious, it is one that is often overlooked. There is actually a good reason it is overlooked. You are in your position of leadership because you were really good at what you *did*. You *were* a powerful doer and executed regularly. *Now* you are leader and your natural inclination is to continue *to do*.

If you are like most people, you do not have the liberty of being a leader exclusively. This means that you will still have a job to do as well as leadership responsibilities. We call this a working leader. Because you are a working leader, it is easy to get caught up in the whirlwind of what you have *to do*. You don't often find yourself in situations where you are sitting at a desk wondering, "Hmm, what should I do today?" We are all busy and have things to do. As a result, leading takes a backseat.

You need to give yourself permission to lead. All of my clients have a boss that has brought me or my company in to help develop his or her leaders. The boss knows that I will be working with the leaders for two hours every month. That adds up to a lot of work time. When I start new engagements, it is not uncommon for my clients to express concern over having the time to work with me for two hours per month. I reassure them that it won't be adding to their load. Coaching actually allows them to process what they are doing and do it more efficiently and effectively. I also tell them that their boss is giving them *permission* to spend that time with me.

You need to give yourself permission to lead on a regular basis. It is always worth the time. Give yourself permission to lead vs. do, do, do. We *do* because it is easy, and we know how. It is comfortable for us. When we *do*, we feel a sense of accomplishment. We can show we are busy.

When it comes to leadership, we have to intentionally add some tools to our toolbox and use those tools.

I had been coaching Heather for a while when she was contacted by a recruiter for a new position of leadership. Our coaching shifted to whether this was the right opportunity for her. Because Heather was *accelerating her leadership growth* with coaching, she was *promoted* by being hired to this new company.

Heather was hired as the new CEO of a company with 1,100 employees. We discussed her first 90 days and how to maximize this new opportunity. One of her early goals was to spend a day meeting with employees at each of the two main locations. She wanted to let them meet her and see she was real and that she cared for them. She was uncovering the human element.

The two days Heather spent at the sites went just as she had hoped.

She met a number of employees and she felt that they were receptive and happy to have her as their new leader. She had food brought in, and the employees met Heather as a person, not just as the new CEO. Several of the employees were shocked that the head of the company would take the time to meet them and be open to questions. Most employees, however, had hoped for and expected the visit from their new leader.

A month later we were discussing Heather returning to the locations for the same purpose. We discussed why this second trip would be so crucial. The first visit was *expected*. Every new CEO makes the rounds to the people in their organization. The second visit is not expected by most employees and is therefore powerful. Heather made the second round of visits, and this created the perception that things were different, and the employees mattered. The team at the top cared about them. This is just one strategy that Heather executed. She is doing a great job, and her organization is reaping the benefits.

Heather was intentional in her leadership. For you to be successful as a leader, you need to be intentional as well.

At the beginning of our engagements with clients, we regularly hear certain phrases. As we begin to dig into their roles and companies, we hear phrases like, "I hope things get better." "I think things will change." "Once I get my next hire, we will be effective." "If I only had a different boss…."

I understand where these leaders are coming from, but I quickly repeat these phrases back to them. I want them to hear what they are saying. Then I draw out this point:

Hope is not leadership. If things are going to improve, you have to intentionally lead to bring the company to a better place. If you are waiting for the next hire, you are delaying building your current team to their fullest capacity. Why not build them up now so that when the new hire comes on board, he or she enters a powerful and effective team? If you wait for things to change, they may never change. Be a change agent, and make it happen now! That is intentional leadership.

Tim Kight, the founder and CEO of Focus 3 (www.focus3.com), has put this concept into a phrase that is powerful. He describes our tendency to do what is natural, easy and effortless. These are our default responses. This is seen at work with behaviors like blaming others or skirting responsibility and ownership. These are our default responses. It is default in the sense that we fall back to these as natural and normal.

Intentional leadership does not live in the world of default. Intentional leadership is disciplined and focused. This is where we wake up ready to make a difference and do what is right, not just what is easy. Tim has created this little graphic to illustrate the two.

Above the Line - DISCIPLINE

Below the Line - DEFAULT

With this graphic, you can ask yourself these questions every day: Am I living above the line today? Am I choosing to be intentional, disciplined and maximizing my impact? Or, am I falling back into what is natural and easy, my default patterns? Discipline or Default?

This is intentional leadership.

Here are a few areas in which you can be intentional in your leadership.

Follow your leadership intuition.

Chris was a very good leader. He was actually a much better leader than he realized. Like many of our clients, he had great intuition. During our coaching sessions, Chris would describe different situations going on with his team. I would often ask what he felt he needed to do to lead through these issues. Without fail, Chris always had a great response.

I would then ask him what he was *going* to do. Catch this, he had great intuition and laid out a great plan of how to lead his people through things. The question was whether he was going to act on his intuition. Historically, he would not act. Chris would stand by and *hope* things would change. We now know, hope is not leadership.

With some encouraging words and a pleasant push from me, Chris would realize his intuition was good and he should act on it. This occurred numerous times throughout our coaching engagement. Chris finally developed the habit of being intentional and acting on his leadership intuition. He began getting some small wins, then big wins, under his belt. As you can imagine, this created more confidence to follow his intuition.

What is the result? Chris has accelerated his leadership growth and is now impacting his company in a larger way. I had the opportunity to lead a workshop for the senior leaders at his organization. I praised him in front of his colleagues and boss for his outstanding leadership intuition. I even challenged the others to run things by him and see how powerful his insights are.

This is intentional leadership.

Treat everyone fairly, not equally.

The G.O.A.L had a team of twelve. He invested time with this group and prepared them to lead a revolution. He was very intentional in his leadership. Of the twelve, he was closer to three of them. He did not neglect the other nine, but he did spend more time with the three. They had integral parts to play, and he gave them what they needed to be successful. Of those three, he had a special relationship with one of them. This one was not a favorite, but he was like a best friend and the closest of all the twelve. He would play a special role in the execution of the world-wide mission.

The G.O.A.L taught us this: treat everybody fairly, but not equally. He made sure that his entire team was set up for success, but there were some on the team who were more gifted or committed, and they deserved to be put in a position to accomplish more. Everyone was treated fairly but not equally. Some deserved the opportunity for more exposure and leadership.

As a leader and as a human, you have the privilege of impacting others with your leadership. You need to treat everyone fairly. They deserve this because they are humans, just like you. You do not need to treat them equally. When you encounter a team member that is willing to put in extra effort and hours, you should give her more responsibility. When you see someone that is creative and identifying new opportunities, you need to let him take ownership and try executing those ideas. When that new team member comes to you asking questions about things that are outside the scope of her responsibility, listen to her. Listen to understand her and identify how you can set her up for success. Even if it means sending her to another part of the organization. Even if it means she leaves and joins another organization.

This is a difficult concept, and the first time you read this, you may not like it or believe it. This is understandable. Read the three paragraphs above again and consider the concept for a moment. Read the paragraphs a third time and begin thinking about the people that make up your team, your direct reports. Are there some that excel? Are there some that go the extra mile? Do you see one that could be your successor? If you can visualize the people, you can see this concept come to life.

This is intentional leadership.

Take time to lead.

At the start of this chapter, I explained that most leaders feel they do not have the time to lead. My clients initially feel they do not have the time for coaching. By the time we are concluding our seven to twelve months together, they have formed a new habit. They have formed the habit of taking one hour, every two weeks, to do nothing but think about and develop their leadership.

As we are wrapping up our engagements, I lay a challenge out to our clients. I remind them that they have formed a new habit. They have formed the habit of taking two hours per month developing their leadership craft. I then tell them to populate the next twelve months on their calendar with our bi-weekly sessions.

No, I will not be on the phone with them anymore. However, they can still take this time to think and act as a leader. They can think about their team and the needs of their team. They can consider whom they need to invest more time in. They can evaluate how everyone is growing. They can view things from 30,000 feet. This is where we look at the company and where it is headed. From 20,000 feet we look at how things are getting accomplished. Are we meeting our goals? At 10,000 feet we look at the key players and identify those that need some extra opportunities to lead. We can then go 5,000 feet or less and get into some of the weeds. This allows us to be strategic in how we lead people.

Hear me out on this. The time you spend alone thinking about and developing your leadership will have a larger impact than going out and doing the work. The return on investment of your time is incredible.

Marshall Goldsmith explains this in terms of a payment. He says that as a leader, you are going to pay, and that payment is your time and energy. You are either going to pay now or pay later. If you take the extra time now to explain things to your people and delegate more powerfully, they will rise up and be more productive. You are paying now. On the back-end, you will have more time to do what only you can do because the rest of the team is doing everything else. The other option is to not delegate and develop others. This mode is chosen because it *appears to be* easier and faster to just do it yourself. The problem with this is that you will have to keep doing it over and over because no one else has been developed to do it. You will pay on the back-end and for a long time.

You have a choice in this. Leaders are intentional.

This is intentional leadership.

Consider every conversation as an opportunity to lead.
Randy was a very friendly and gregarious person. He was well-liked and respected at his company. During our sessions, he would share with

me conversations he had with his direct reports, peers, and his boss. Randy could tell a story! I felt like I was involved because of his mastery in setting a scene and describing people's words, moods and actions.

I noticed a trend with Randy. He was the answer man. As he laid out conversation after conversation, it always concluded with what he told that person they needed to do. This is not necessarily a bad thing because often people came to Randy for answers.

Yet, I challenged Randy on this. Why did he always give guidance? Why did he feel he always had the right answer for people? Randy answered my queries by stating that it was his job as a leader to have answers for his people.

I challenged Randy on this even further. Is it your job to have answers for them or is it your job to help them generate and evaluate answers for themselves? Randy fell silent. No response (and this was not normal). He had been viewing these conversations from a transactional basis. They asked, he answered. This is not intentional leadership. Intentional leaders listen to the questions and then ask the people what they think they should do. Be intentional in making it a teaching opportunity.

Randy started doing this. In a later session, he shared his amazement at how smart and creative his team members were. He had always viewed them as capable, but now he viewed them as smart and ingenious. Why? Because he was intentional in listening and helping them find answers for themselves. (More on this in the next chapter with our last strategy).

In every conversation, ask yourself how you can make this a leadership moment. How can this be a time of teaching? Learning? Mentoring? Stop living in the transactional; live in the relational.

This is intentional leadership.

Acknowledge what you know!

During coaching sessions, I ask a lot of questions. Most clients have an answer to the questions. They not only have an answer, they have good answers. I then ask them what they are going to do with what they know. The common response is, "Should I do anything?" *Yes.*

All leaders need to acknowledge what they know or what they are thinking. Share your thoughts and observations to impact others. Do not hold them in because that has no value to others.

Simply, this means to say out loud what you are thinking in your masterful brain.

Kristy was having a difficult time with her employee, Cindy. Cindy had always been smart and productive, but that had changed over the past six months. Her productivity had lapsed, and her engagement diminished. As Kristy was describing the situation to me, she became much more emotional and almost shaken. Part of her frustration was the quality of work. The other part was her frustration in not being able to help Cindy.

I asked Kristy if she was aware of anything that had changed for Cindy from six months ago. Kristy said no. I asked if there were any changes at work? Changes in systems, processes, or personnel? She said no. I asked Kristy to stop for sixty seconds and consider the situation to see if there is something she was missing.

After about forty-five seconds, Kristy began to talk. She shared that two members of Cindy's team had left the company. The new hires that replaced them were more experienced and had higher levels of leadership in their previous organizations. Then Kristy stopped. I asked if there was anything more? She said no. I asked her to think about it and what Cindy *might* be feeling as a result of these changes.

Kristy then speculated that maybe Cindy felt a bit inferior. Maybe Cindy felt that the two new hires did not need her leadership and she was unnecessary. Then Kristy said, "But that is not true! We still need Cindy. We need her even more. If we have two great employees, we want to set them up for success. We want them to stay here and benefit the company. Cindy has a larger role with these two employees, not a smaller role."

I praised Kristy for her insights. Then I told her she needed to have a conversation with Cindy to share everything she just shared with me. Kristy did have that conversation. It was a turning point in their relationship and a turning point in Cindy leading the new employees.

Acknowledge what you know. Share your thoughts. Share the why.

This is intentional leadership.

Now, be intentional and follow the steps below to put this all into action.

ACCELERATE YOUR LEADERSHIP

- Intentionally set one hour for leadership thinking and strategy on your calendar twice a month. Right now. Do it.
- Intentionally consider the things you have hoped will change. Identify what to do about it. Now, do it.
- Intentionally consider your direct reports. Who is your successor? Who will be your inner circle?
- Follow your intuition on a pending decision. Decide and act now.
- Acknowledge what you know by having some open conversations.

This is How I Role

Chapter 7 - Sustain Success with Coaching

Strategy #7: Sustain Success with Coaching

From the moment I began the coaching engagement with Maria, she got it. A high performer in her organization, Maria did not feel like she had a seat at the table. She was on the executive team, but in their meetings, Maria literally was sitting at a smaller table with two others while the rest of the executive team sat at the big table. This physical situation affected her mental state. She did not feel like she had a seat at the big table.

I could tell that Maria had great leadership intuition. I could see that she knew her trade and was a subject matter expert. I knew that her ceiling for leadership was much higher. She needed to see that for herself.

During out meetings together, I would go out of my way to help her see what she was capable of doing and how capable she was of leading. Maria shared how she was leading her team. She delegated well. She inspired them. She modeled the way to others by how she did her own work. As she shared these things, I finally asked her why she could not do the same things with her peers and even her boss, the CEO. Maria liked the idea but was still hesitant. Her approach worked with her team and her direct reports, but would this type of leadership work with peers and her boss? The short answer is yes.

Maria took a few chances with her peers. She went to them with a posture of being inquisitive, not assuming or judgmental. She asked good questions to understand why they did what they did. She opened conversations about how they could be better together instead of in their separate silos. She even went to the CEO to share some observations and have a difficult conversation.

I would like to say that all of these conversations went phenomenally well and worked perfectly. That is not reality. They did start paving the way for new and improved relationships. They did open the eyes of the executive team that Maria had something to share, something to bring to the table. Maria's change in behavior was not an overnight success, but it did make a difference. It took some time, but Maria addressed the physical situation of the executive team meetings. Today, they *all* sit at the same table, right where she belongs.

Can you believe that we are on our last strategy to accelerate your leadership growth and promotability? If you have been diligent and intentional with the first six strategies, we have come to this point of asking, "How do you sustain the growth?" There is a relatively simple answer to the question. You sustain the growth with coaching.

You are now the coach. Your sustained success is based on the sustained success of others, and you sustain their success through coaching.

Lead and influence with coaching. People will not remember you because of your intellect and wise words. People will not remember you because you hit your quotas and metrics. People will remember you for the impact you had on them and the way you made them feel. You impact them by treating them as a human; we are all a part of the human race. You impact them by pulling the best out of them and helping them elevate in their career. This is what coaching does for people. You pull the best out of them. It is still them; it is just them 2.0.

So, what is coaching? Let me give you an overly simplistic definition of coaching: *Turn every statement into a question.*

Coaches ask great questions. Here are some examples from other leaders of common statements and great coaching questions and recommendations to change the conversation.

Statement: I have noticed that you have not met your quota the past two months. I want you to try doing this....

Question: I am sure that you are aware that you have missed your quota lately, why do you think that has happened? What do you think you can do to change the situation?

Statement: You have expressed dissatisfaction with your pay recently. You are paid based on your role and it is competitive with others at this company and with benchmarks from other companies.

Question: You have expressed dissatisfaction with your pay recently. Help me understand why you feel underpaid? What do you think we can do to remedy the situation?

Statement: You are not doing this correctly and it is impacting others. Let me show you how to do it.

Question: You are not doing this correctly. Do you see how this is impacting others? What do you think is the proper way to do this? Why?

Statement: I see a bright future for you. Here are the steps you should take to move up in the organization.

Question: I see a bright future for you. Do you desire to move up in the organization? In what area? What do you see as the necessary steps to prepare you for that move? How can I help you get there?

All of these are real examples shared by my clients. As simple as this sounds, asking questions conflicts with the way we have been taught to lead. As leaders, we feel that we have to the have answers. *Overcome that feeling and let your people find their own answers.*

This is important. If you provide all the answers, you take responsibility for your employees' situations. They will implement what you said, and if it does not work, they will look back to you as the reason it did not work. They will also come back to you for the next answer. They need to own their stuff. They need to own their situations. They need to own their growth. Let them find the answers in themselves, and you set them up for success.

As a leader, you should be having regular one-on-one (1:1) conversations with your direct reports. Turn these 1:1 meetings into coaching sessions. Make your 1:1 conversations much more than checking boxes and working through the technical issues. The technical is important, but take it to the next level by dealing with strategy and development. This leads to constant growth that is sustainable for the long term.

You will be amazed at the answers your team members provide to your questions. Their answers will help you identify ways to tap into their intrinsic motivations. You will see how you can challenge them. You will actually learn from them. I know this seems crazy, but if you listen to their answers, your team members will share insights that benefit you also. This is a win-win scenario.

The G.O.A.L. was a fantastic coach, and he used the principle of turning statements into questions. People came to him with questions on a regular basis. He would ponder their questions and then turn the tables on them. When they finished their question, he would respond by asking them what they think? What have they been taught previously? What do they see as the best solution to the problem? Many times, they would still be at a loss and he would have them go away and ponder the situation and then come back to him. If it worked for The G.O.A.L., it will work for you.

How do I start coaching?

There are plenty of coaching schools you could attend. These are valuable, but they also come with an investment. This might be a logical step for you. All these programs will teach you various models for coaching. I have created one that I use with a number of clients. This is also very simple, but not easy. It is a great place to start and a place you can start right now.

This is my DOC model of coaching. Doctors are known for their ability to diagnose a situation by asking seven questions that help them pinpoint the issue. In the same way, this model will help you lead your people to success and growth.

Discover

Start your coaching by asking good questions and discover what is happening. We start by turning every statement into a question. We work to help others discover what they need to do to lead through a situation.

I was in a coaching session earlier today with Brian. Brian has been working to develop a new leadership structure for his company. He was sharing some of the pitfalls of the current structure and why he felt a new structure was needed. I asked him questions about the current structure and where it was falling short. I asked him if the current structure needed replacing or if he needed to make some small adjustments.

As Brian provided answers, he began to gain some clarity and realized that a new structure had to be put in place for long-term success. This discovery process was affirming his intuition. Brian talked through the issue and came to his own conclusions. I did not give him advice. I did not tell him what to do. As an outsider, I have no idea what the right answer is for Brian or his company. He came to his own conclusions through powerful questions and reflective listening on my part, his coach.

Outline

Once we have helped someone discover what is happening or what they need to do, we begin the process of *outlining* how they will get where they need to go. The discover portion helped them see *what* needs to happen. During the outline portion, you help them see *how* it takes place.

This is such an important step. A mistake many leaders make is thinking that since the "what" is uncovered, the employee will know how to do it. These are two separate things. If you help them discover, but neglect to help them outline the steps, there is a great likelihood that they will not execute on what they discovered.

Brian and I continued our session. Since Brian had discovered that a new structure was necessary, I asked him where he needed to start in creating it. Initially he said that he would share his awareness with the president and ask the president how he thought the organization should be structured. I asked Brian if the structure was his responsibility. He said yes. I asked him why he was not taking the first pass at it. He sat silently for a moment.

Brian finally said, "I need to do this, don't I?" I asked him, "Do you?" "Yes," he said. Brian started talking and taking notes for himself. Here is what he came up with:

1. He needed to create a visual of the new leadership structure with the titles and names of people that would fill each position. Brian realized that some of the positions would need to be new hires.

2. Brian acknowledged that he needed to create the plan with powerful talking points to take to his president and the board of directors. These leaders would have to sign off for the change to happen.

3. Brian looked at the current employees and identified some areas they would need to develop to be effective in new roles. He realized the need to coach them so they could develop some new skills in order to be successful.

4. He needed to create a communication plan and enact some change management skills so that the transition to the new structure would be successful. Brian felt part of this would be a question and answer session with those who were directly affected.

This list may not be a complete and comprehensive view of what Brian needs to outline to implement the new structure, but it is a powerful start. He came up with it himself in the course of twenty minutes. He had it in him; it was my job to ask good questions to pull it out of him. That is the power of good questions. Have your employees outline the necessary steps and they take ownership of the situation.

Challenge

Now that we have coached our people to *discover* the what and *outline* the how, it is time to *challenge* them to start. This is critical. According to *Fortune*, nine out of ten organizations fail to implement their strategic plan. This is at the organizational level. It is also reflected in individuals. Failure to launch on a plan is real.

Whether a plan is large or small, there has to be a challenge to get started. As a coach, I have a responsibility to challenge my clients. It is my job to stretch them out of their comfort zone because that is where growth takes place. As a leader, when you coach your team members, you have the same responsibility for the same reason.

As Brian wrapped up discussing the steps he needed to take, I asked him what he was going to do first. He thought about it and said that he needed to create the visual and the story and then take it to the president. I asked him how long he felt he needed to create the visual and story. Brian thought he could do it within one week because a lot of it was already laid out.

I asked him if he would email me the visual and structure in a week. I do not need to review and approve it; I was challenging him and holding him accountable to see that he executed. I asked him when he would present it to the president to get some initial feedback. Brian said that would happen during their 1:1 the week after he completed the plan. Since Brian and I meet every other week, I told him that I looked forward to hearing how the meeting went and the reaction of the president.

Brian was excited at this point. He had a plan laid out with some concrete steps to move forward and the timing to get it done. He did not feel overwhelmed or weak. He felt informed, empowered and energized.

I did not tell him what or how, he did it on his own. That is the power of coaching.

This is a simple model: DOC. Simple works. Get your feet wet and try it during your next 1:1 with a direct report. It works in meetings with peers. It works with your boss. Try the approach and then evaluate for yourself what worked and did not work. See how you might approach a conversation differently the next time. Be agile and make adjustments as you go. If you are looking to sustain your success and the success of others, coaching is the key.

Remember Maria from the start of the chapter? She has continued to share her thoughts and feelings. She is leading her team well. She is leading across to her peers. She has had some incredible conversations with the CEO, and he now seeks her out for advice. I attended a conference last week for Maria's organization. She was one of many who were sharing from the stage that day. It was a pleasure to stand back and watch her speak with confidence, authority and grace. At the end, one of her colleagues came up to me and said what a breath of fresh air Maria is in the organization. She said that in the past year Maria has changed. She said Maria used to sit back and watch and not speak up. Now, she says that Maria speaks up, encourages others, and impacts the entire organization. I smiled and affirmed the comments. Inside I was thinking that this is the real Maria, and she has finally come out of her shell. She was coachable, and she realized her potential.

I still work with Maria. Now she is asking me the questions. She wants to go through formal coach training and impact people around the country, not just in her organization. I do not know what the future holds for her. I do know that because she has caught the coaching bug, she and those she leads will have sustained growth.

When you lead intentionally and implement the strategies we have discussed, you will have great success for years to come.

It is time to role on.

ACCELERATE YOUR LEADERSHIP

- Put on your coaching hat with your direct reports. Turn every statement into a question.
- Schedule regular 1:1 meetings with your team and coach them to success.
- Use the DOC model and make adjustments as you move forward.
- Invest in your people today.

This is How I Role

Chapter 8 - Still Role-ing On

So those are the seven strategies. While plenty more could be shared (look for the sequel), these are a great place to start. Here is the huge question you need to ask yourself: *Now what?* What am I going to do with this information? What am I going to do today to accelerate my leadership journey?

Start today! Too many people waste energy wondering where to begin. They think about it, and think about it, and think about it and never actually start. Get started. You will never move forward in your journey without taking the first step.

For you to be a great leader of others, you have to lead yourself first. Put in the time and develop your skills. Self-leadership takes you to another level where you can influence others.

Andy has been in a leadership position for a number of years. His company brought us in because his direct reports were not growing. They were able to execute but they were not impacting the company at the level the senior leaders desired. During my personal deep dive with Andy, I realized that he had reached the height of his career, at least in his own eyes. His goal had always been to be a manager. He did not desire anything higher than that for himself or others.

The result of this mentality was stagnation for him and the people he was blessed to lead. You never "arrive" in leadership. It is constant growth, progression, learning and development. If you feel you have arrived and stop the process, you will begin to fall backwards. You are either moving forward or backward; there is no such thing as staying the same.

Because Andy felt he had arrived, he was no longer striving to move forward. He became satisfied with the status quo. I asked him what "arriving" looked like for him. He had stopped reading books. He stopped striving for what was next in his career and stopped leading himself. Andy was in full "take it day-to-day" mode.

I asked Andy how his approach was impacting the people he was leading. He stopped, contemplated the question, and finally responded by saying, "I have no idea." He had no idea because he never considered how pressing the pause button on his own growth would negatively impact his people.

Let me interrupt this story about Andy for a moment. I am not one that thinks there is always more, and you need to go 110 miles per hour in your career. When you are promoted, you need to spend time learning at the new level. You should enjoy the journey and your new position for a period of time. Learn all you can without looking too far ahead and missing the opportunities for growth. As long as you are learning and not coasting, it is good to spend a year or two (or three) in each role.

Back to Andy. Through our work together, Andy came to the realization that he had to lead himself if he was going to lead others. He reignited his leadership journey and began developing his skills so that he could pass them on to his team. It was not an overnight shift for him, but he got there.

Fast-forward three months and Andy's entire mindset had changed. He came to the realization that there was more for him. Simply being a manager was no longer enough. He wanted to move up and impact even more people in profound ways.

Andy is on that journey now. He is working and developing his skills as a leader. His boss has noticed this change in attitude and behavior and likes what he sees. What is the ceiling on Andy's career? I have no idea. I do know that as long as he continues to grow, develop and lead himself, his impact on others will be substantial.

Role-ing on is something I focus on regularly. I want to lead myself in a powerful way so that I can lead others. *Even though I am a coach, I am constantly learning. Remember: leaders are learners.* It seems that I learn more from my clients than they learn from me. These mutually beneficial relationships help me get up every morning and go after it.

Let me give you a few examples of how I am role-ing on. I hired a book coach to help me with this book. I have never written a book before. I have wanted to for a long time. I have had mentors that said, "Everyone has book inside." I wanted to write one, but I knew I needed help. After some research and vetting, I hired Bonnie Budzowski from InCredible Messages.

Bonnie has been so powerful in helping establish the strategy for the book. We spent hours on the phone with her asking me questions and coaching me to pull the book out of me. It was fun for me to be on the other side of coaching. She has been a support throughout the process (which was much more difficult than I ever imagined). She has provided constructive feedback after each chapter was completed. She looked over the completed work and gave some final thoughts for edits and changes. You would not be reading this today if I had not hired Bonnie.

I know the importance of bringing others into my life so that I get better. As a leader, I practice what I preach. There were many others that helped make this book a reality; you can read about them in the acknowledgments.

There are coaches that I admire who have businesses much larger than mine. I talk with them. I pick their brains. I find nuggets of wisdom that I can use to develop my coaching skills and coaching business. I do not have all the answers. I do not need to have all of the answers. I just need to know people, and talk with people, who have the answers. When these coaches share insights and perspective, I act on it. To seek input is great. To act on it is where the growth takes place.

As the business has grown, I have come to the realization that I am navigating into unchartered waters for me. Later this year I am attending a conference geared towards business owners and entrepreneurs. This is a financial and time investment for me, but it is a step I need to take. This conference will have quality content to help me learn how to scale effectively while maintaining our brand. I will learn what strategic positions I need to create to continue the current rate of growth. As with most conferences, the people I meet and the relationships I develop will be half of the benefit. The attendees will all be similar to me. I know that I will find a few business owners that are one, two, or three steps ahead of me on the journey and they will help me get where I want to go.

What separates the great leaders from average leaders? They work it. They execute. No one can do it for you.

Legendary NFL player, coach, commentator, author and speaker Tony Dungy said, "Expectations! Execution! No Excuses! No Explanation!" This is a great quote. This is how you win as a leader and how you win in life. Stick with me as I take Dungy's quote and break it down in how it applies to role-ing on.

Expectations! You have to want it. You have to take control of your own career and set expectations for yourself. This is not only for your career, but even for your current role in leadership. I was launching a new coaching engagement last month and my client, Nikki, shared something that I hear quite often. She said that she is not sure what success looks like because her boss has not articulated clear expectations.

I asked Nikki if she had expectations for what she wanted to accomplish and for what she wanted from her team. She did. When I asked her to share them with me, Nikki laid out a powerful list of expectations and metrics. I asked her if she had shared these with her boss. She had not. She then said (unprompted from me) that she was going to go share them with her boss that day. She did. He loved them.

I encourage you to set leadership expectations and go. That is how you role! Don't wait around for somebody to do this for you.

Execution! As a leader, you need to make sure that things are getting done. You are blessed as a leader that you get things done with and through others, but it is still on you to make sure things get done. Execute at a high level. Often the thing stopping us from execution is making decisions. If we do not decide what we are going to do and how we are going to execute it, we will never move the ball forward.

During a recent coaching session, I asked David how his team project was moving forward. He said that nothing had happened over the past month. Things were stalled and it was going to take a bit longer than expected to complete the project. I asked David some questions: Why was the project delayed? When did his team last meet about the project? How had the meeting gone?

David didn't know why the project was delayed, even though the team had met the day before. The team had spent an hour going over all the things that needed to happen. They had some productive conflict on some of the elements. David's team was ready to go.

I asked David if the meeting finished with each team member having something to accomplish. A task. Something tangible so that they could execute. By a specific date.

David said that the team had tabled the discussion until the following month because they could not come to any decisions.

It is important to have everyone on the same page and be intentional in moving forward. But you can't stop there. It is also important to execute. Football teams will never score if all they do is huddle. They execute the play that is called in the huddle and that is how they win. Execution! That is how you role!

No Excuses! This one is plain and simple. Stop telling yourself why you cannot do something. Start figuring out to how to get it done. Lead through obstacles. Do not let obstacles become excuses for failing to lead to results. A team that I have been coaching has been so creative in letting me know why things are not getting done. I could take a transcript from my sessions with this team and write a book called *1000 Excuses to Destroy Getting Results!*

We got to a point with this team where I had to repeat the plethora of excuses and ask them if they were ever going to tell me how they *could* move forward. The message got through that day but still no results. I am on the fence if they will ever get there.

Excuses create a culture where you come up with more excuses. To overcome this, you need to call it out and refuse to accept excuses. When you move from excuses to solutions, you will get results. That is how you role!

No Explanation! This is very similar to the previous point. In most situations, an explanation is just an excuse tied up in pretty and flowery language. No explanation needed here. See above. That is how you role!

So, what is the key to role-ing on and continuously improving? It is common in coaching sessions for clients to complain about their boss. Most people feel that they do not have a good role model in their own boss (kind of sounds like an excuse). I ask my client what characteristics they think would define an effective leader. It is crazy that it usually takes some time for them to answer this question. We do not naturally think of the qualities we would want from someone leading us, but we know when those qualities aren't there. Eventually, I usually get responses such as:

- Honest
- Cares about me
- Develops my skills
- Gives me opportunities to grow
- Consistent
- Reliable
- Subject matter expert
- Decisive
- Driven

What would you add to this list?

These are outstanding qualities that we all want in our leaders. Once my complaining clients have generated a similar list, I turn the tables on them with one exhortation: *Be the leader that you want to follow.* You know what you want in a leader; be that leader. If honesty and integrity top your list, lead with the utmost honesty and integrity. If reliability is important to you, make sure you show up on time and do what you say you will do. If you want to follow a driven leader, be driven in your work and how you lead. Be the leader that you want to follow.

The G.O.A.L had a concept similar to this. He said to treat others the way that you want to be treated. When we lead the way and model how to do things, people will begin to respond to us in the same way. How we behave. How we care. How we invest in others. Set the pace in these things and others will begin to follow that same path.

It is time. It is *your* time. Life and leadership are a journey. Enjoy the journey and take others along with you. Remember that leadership is about people. You have people around you every day who are looking to be led. Be that leader. Be intentional and strive to impact people along the way. Create a culture and impact people in a way that when they look back on their career, they will remember *you* because you invested in them and made their life better. Live out the strategies in this book and you will be remembered accordingly.

The seven strategies in this book stand on their own, but they also have a bit of sequence to them. You do not need to work through them one by one. You will be working these strategies simultaneously and even going back and forth based on the situation. In learning these strategies, start at the beginning and make your way through. Then you will use them, as needed, based on the situation.

Let's review the strategies and set you up for success.

Strategy #1: Uncover the Human Element. We need to be mindful of our humanity and the humanity of our colleagues. We are all the same. We all have feelings of inadequacy and the need to measure up. Because we are the same, let's give one another some grace and work effectively.

Strategy #2: Manage Processes. Lead People. As we go about our work every day, we need to manage the processes or how we do things. We cannot manage people, we need to lead them. If you try to manage them, it will seem like you are putting your thumb on them and holding back the best they have to offer. When you lead your team members, you are removing barriers and setting them up for success.

Strategy #3: Practice People Whispering. As leaders, we need to develop a connection with our people. Do a personal deep dive and get to know who they are, how they operate and how you can maximize their impact. As the leader, you need to be open and vulnerable with them. People will follow you when they know you.

Strategy #4: Win with T.E.A.M. Business is accomplished in teams today. As the leader, you need to be prepared to take your team(s) to the next level. You do this by establishing a baseline of trust and bringing the energy every day to push your team forward. When you lead effectively, the team will hold themselves accountable to accomplish the task. Finally, you keep them all focused on the mission. This is the team mission and their personal missions.

Strategy #5 – Learn the New Scorecard. As a leader, you are no longer evaluated the way that you always have been. You need to shift your thinking and realize that the old metrics of success no longer apply. It is not about how many sales you made or projects you completed. It is about the team you are leading. Are they elevating their game? Are they set up for success? Their success is your success.

Strategy #6 – Lead with Intention. Everything, yes, everything, in leadership needs to be intentional. You need to set aside time and block your calendar to think about leadership. You need to focus and ask yourself how you are leading. Hope is not leadership. You must be intentional. When you are, great growth will occur in you and your team.

Strategy #7 – Sustain Success with Coaching. As a leader, you need to be a coach. Consistently invest in your people and coach them to success. Our simple model is the DOC model. Discover what is happening with great questions. Outline the steps with them that will help them succeed. Challenge them to execute and cross the finish line.

Use the seven strategies to accelerate your leadership growth and promotability. I know you can, and when you do, I want to hear your story. When you have implemented some or all of these strategies and you have moved up, tell me and my team about it. Send your stories to **Thisishowirole@renogize.com.**

We will follow up with you personally to congratulate you and learn from you. Your story may be in the follow-up to this book!

If this book has sparked an interest in coaching and leadership development for you, reach out to us. It would be a pleasure to have a conversation with you or your company and see how we can come in and walk alongside you. Developing yourself is not just about being a better leader, this is about making a difference. It is about impacting lives. We would be honored to help you on that journey.

ACCELERATE YOUR LEADERSHIP

- Be a leader.
- Be intentional.
- You can do it.
- Start now.

This is How I Role

Acknowledgments

There are so many people that have made this book possible. This entire experience has been much more difficult than I ever imagined.

To my incredible wife, Jen, thank you for standing by me in this. Your words of encouragement when I questioned my ability to do this were tremendous. Your content review and ideas were so beneficial. Helping make "how I speak" come across in print was not easy, but you did it. You have been my life-long partner and my partner in this book journey. Thank you, I love you.

To my daughter, Sydney, thank you for listening to constant conversations about the book at the dinner table. Thank you for editing content and making sure what I said made sense. Thank you for always being a support and helping push me across the finish line. You are awesome, squirt.

My book coach, Bonnie Budzowski, you have been a blessing. Your steady hand and guidance when I felt this was beyond me were powerful. Your keen ability to draw my book out of me and put some structure around my thoughts has resulted in this work. Thank you for all of your help and support in the process.

Thank you to Sarah Starkey for stepping out of your role as a Junior High English teacher and editing my work. Lorraine Entwisle, you went above and beyond. You were a final line of editing, laid out the book in Amazon, created the cover with us and encouraged us to keep going. Cheryl Jackson, thank you for sharing your great smile and attitude as the model for our cover.

There are so many who have helped me on my leadership journey and challenged me to write a book. Thank you to Ivor Davies, Jeff Underwood, Sam Smith, Scott Osborne, Caroline Dowd-Higgins and Steve Kovich. Thank you to all of my amazing clients, you are really friends. You teach me more than you know. It is an honor to work with you all.

About the Author

Sean Olson is an executive coach, facilitator and keynote speaker with over 25 years of experience helping individuals, teams and companies reach their full potential and effectiveness. He has worked with officers, directors and senior managers in start-ups to Fortune 500 companies.

As an executive coach, Sean works with individuals and teams from the C-Suite to Managers. His business background and relational skills work to bring powerful results for his clients. He works most effectively with individuals and teams that are looking to move rapidly and are ready to put in the work necessary to change.

As a leadership facilitator, Sean delivers workshops on Teamwork, Strategy Development, Work Styles, Company Culture, Conflict Management, and Emotional Intelligence. He has also led seminars on Group Coaching and Coaching for Impact. His reviews from speaking often highlight how interactive and engaging he is with the audience.

Sean is an Associate Certified Coach (ACC) with the International Coaching Federation. He is also a Marshall Goldsmith Executive Coaching Stakeholder-Centered Coach. He has served on the program committee for the Indianapolis chapter of ICF and the program committee for the ICF Midwest Regional Conference. He has also completed the CoachU Core Competency Program and is completing the Advanced Corporate CoachU program. Sean also holds his Bachelor's and Master of Arts Degrees.

Sean enjoys sharing life with his wife, Jen, and daughter, Sydney. Together they enjoy cooking, traveling, basketball and impacting others.

Your Next Steps with Sean Olson
and Renogize Professional Coaching

Do you have the desire and drive to take your career to the next level? Are you ready to become the leader that you have always desired to be? Is it time for your company to outshine the competition with leaders that execute?

If the answer is yes, then Renogize Professional Coaching is your partner. We work with companies to turn good leaders into *great* leaders. We do this through:

- One-on-One Executive Coaching
- Team Coaching
- Group Coaching
- Leadership Workshops
- Fully Customized Leadership Development Programs
- Leadership Assessments
- Keynote Speaking

If you think Renogize Professional Coaching may be a good fit for you, we would like to have a conversation with you about your needs. You can visit our website at www.Renogize.com, email us at info@renogize.com or call us at 812-219-8273.

Renogize Professional Coaching has a team of coaches around the country ready to help you. We are a mission-driven business. 33% of our annual profits benefit charities that focus on faith, leadership and education.

Made in the USA
Coppell, TX
03 February 2021